Access to History
General Editor: Keith Randell

Tories, Conservatives and Unionists 1815-1914

Duncan Watts

Hodder & Stoughton
A MEMBER OF THE HODDER HEADLINE GROUP

The cover illustration is a portrait of Benjamin Disraeli by Weigall.
(Courtesy of Private Collection/Bridgeman Art Library.)

Some other titles in the series:

Labour and Reform: Working Class Movements 1815-1914   ISBN 0 340 52930 X
Clive Behagg

Britain: Foreign and Imperial Affairs 1919-39   ISBN 0 340 55928 4
Alan Farmer

Britain: Domestic Politics 1918-39   ISBN 0 340 55647 1
Robert Pearce

Britain: Foreign and Imperial Affairs 1939-64   ISBN 0 340 59256 7
Alan Farmer

Britain: Domestic Politics 1939-64   ISBN 0 340 59702 X
Paul Adelman

The Concert of Europe: International Relations 1814-70   ISBN 0 340 53496 6
John Lowe

British Library Cataloguing in Publication Data

A catalogue for this book is
available from the British Library

ISBN 0-340-60081-0

First published 1994

Impression number   10 9 8 7 6 5 4
Year   1998 1997

© 1994 Duncan Watts

Typeset by Sempringham publishing, Bedford
Printed in Great Britain for Hodder & Stoughton Educational, a division of Hodder
Headline Plc, 338 Euston Road, London NW1 3BH by
Redwood Books, Trowbridge, Wiltshire

Contents

Preface

To the general reader

Although the *Access to History* series has been designed with the needs of students studying the subject at higher examination levels very much in mind, it also has a great deal to offer the general reader. The main body of the text (i.e. ignoring the Study Guides at the ends of chapters) forms a readable and yet stimulating survey of a coherent topic as studied by historians. However, each author's aim has not merely been to provide a clear explanation of what happened in the past (to interest and inform): it has also been assumed that most readers wish to be stimulated into thinking further about the topic and to form opinions of their own about the significance of the events that are described and discussed (to be challenged). Thus, although no prior knowledge of the topic is expected on the reader's part, she or he is treated as an intelligent and thinking person throughout. The author tends to share ideas and possibilities with the reader, rather than passing on numbers of so-called 'historical truths'.

To the student reader

There are many ways in which the series can be used by students studying History at a higher level. It will, therefore, be worthwhile thinking about your own study strategy before you start your work on this book. Obviously, your strategy will vary depending on the aim you have in mind, and the time for study that is available to you.

If, for example, you want to acquire a general overview of the topic in the shortest possible time, the following approach will probably be the most effective:

1 Read chapter 1 and think about its contents.
2 Read the 'Making notes' section at the end of chapter 2 and decide whether it is necessary for you to read this chapter.
3 If it is, read the chapter, stopping at each heading to note down the main points that have been made.
4 Repeat stage 2 (and stage 3 where appropriate) for all the other chapters.

If, however, your aim is to gain a thorough grasp of the topic, taking however much time is necessary to do so, you may benefit from carrying out the same procedure with each chapter, as follows:

1 Read the chapter as fast as you can, and preferably at one sitting.
2 Study the flow diagram at the end of the chapter, ensuring that you understand the general 'shape' of what you have just read.

3 Read the 'Making notes' section (and the 'Answering essay questions' section, if there is one) and decide what further work you need to do on the chapter. In particularly important sections of the book, this will involve reading the chapter a second time and stopping at each heading to think about (and to write a summary of) what you have just read.
4 Attempt the 'Source-based questions' section. It will sometimes be sufficient to think through your answers, but additional understanding will often be gained by forcing yourself to write them down.

When you have finished the main chapters of the book, study the 'Further Reading' section and decide what additional reading (if any) you will do on the topic.

This book has been designed to help make your studies both enjoyable and successful. If you can think of ways in which this could have been done more effectively, please write to tell me. In the meantime, I hope that you will gain greatly from your study of History.

Keith Randell

Acknowledgements

The Publishers would like to thank the following for permission to reproduce illustrations in this volume:

Courtesy of a Private Collection / Bridgeman Art Library, cover.
Punch Publications, pages 64, 119 and 138.

Every effort has been made to trace and acknowledge ownership of copyright. The Publishers will be glad to make suitable arrangements with any copyright holders whom it has not been possible to contact.

CHAPTER 1

Introduction

Political activity in Britain today is firmly based upon the party system. The conduct of political life revolves around political parties, for they are an essential part of every stage of the democratic process, and representative government is unimaginable without them. They act as the vital intermediary between government and the governed.

Every MP has been elected because of his or her party label, and it is often said that the qualities and person of an individual candidate make little difference to the outcome, perhaps being worth no more than one or two per cent of the votes. Most voters are much less interested in the individual who represents them than in their party label, although few would probably go as far as the Midland voter in 1951 who, when interviewed, remarked that he 'would vote for a pig if the party put one up'. Even in elections to choose local councillors, party politics has now come to play a dominant part.

Within the House of Commons party lines are clearly drawn and voting on the vast majority of occasions is conducted on a strictly party basis. Such is the rigidity of party discipline that the Whips can often predict with great precision the outcome of a vote. This is partly because considerable pressure is habitually applied in order to bring any recalcitrant party members into line. Such organisation of political activity within the House of Commons is paralleled by the network of party associations which exist around the country. Fighting elections and maintaining support is an expensive business which requires a highly professional approach, so that these organisations have been developed to raise funds, to encourage support through political activity, and to mobilise the voters to turn-out on polling day.

Yet this was not always the case, for in the early nineteenth century parties were only in their infancy and the party system was yet to be properly established. Indeed, as late as 1864 the philosopher and Radical MP, John Stuart Mill, could write a book about representative government in which parties were not even mentioned! The contrast between British politics today and political life in the early nineteenth century is thus very marked.

1 The Growth of Parties and the Party System

Edmund Burke, a key figure in the development of conservative thought, and himself an MP until his death in 1797, welcomed the idea of political parties and provided us with a classic definition of a party. He described it as 'a body of men united, for promoting by their joint endeavours the national interest, upon some particular principle in which they are all agreed'. Today we recognise that this is still the case, although there are differences of emphasis and degree within parties, and stress the common desire of members to pursue and achieve power in order to accomplish certain things. By a party, then, we mean a body of people who join together and broadly agree upon some general principles, and who seek to implement them by achieving power via periodic elections.

Political parties, in the form of the Whigs and the Tories, can be traced back to the seventeenth century, although, as we shall see, the notion of parties is difficult to apply in eighteenth-century political life, and in the early nineteenth century many people were still unsure about their desirability. Even then they frowned on any attempt to divide people into two groups and saw party as 'faction', something very unpatriotic and disloyal. In as much as they existed, parties were not separated by a fundamental disagreement over political ideals, nor did they represent very different social backgrounds. They were loosely held together, often as a result of historical and family ties, and differed only in their general approach to matters of policy - the Tories being more reluctant to embrace change and the Whigs being a little less fearful of innovation.

Many MPs in 1815 did not class themselves as belonging to either grouping. They considered themselves to be Independents. However, there were many cliques and factions, which were seen as either generally friendly towards the government or as generally opposed to it. The Tories were only able to remain in office until 1830 by winning the backing of enough of these factions and of these unaligned members to secure a majority in the important votes. In the 1830s the division between the parties became more clear-cut, and the two-party system began to function, with Whigs on the one side, and Tories (or Conservatives, as the Peelite party was known), on the other. There followed a period of confusion and instability after the Conservative Party broke up over the repeal of the Corn Laws in 1846, but by 1867 the two-party system had reasserted itself. Thereafter, Conservative and Liberal administrations succeeded each other, normally without having to think about the need for third party support as they were able to form a strong administration with a clear majority in the House.

In 1882, W.S. Gilbert was able to write the famous lines of his popular comic opera *Iolanthe* which pinpointed the basic divide in English politics.

> I often think it's comical
> How often nature does contrive
> That every boy and every girl,
> That's born into the world alive,
> Is either a little Liberal,
> Or else a little Conservative!

In essence he was broadly correct, although, of course, there were other groups and parties at various times, such as Radicals, Peelites and Liberal Unionists.

2 The Conservative Place in the Two-Party System

On the continent, where there tends to be more political parties, parliamentary assemblies are designed differently to our own House of Commons. Seating is arranged in a semi-circular chamber and representatives sit according to their political affiliation - more conservative ones to the right, more radical ones (who in various degrees favour change) to the left. This has given rise to the terms 'Right' and 'Left' which are commonly used in this country. The party of the Left in nineteenth-century Britain was the Liberal Party, and the Conservative Party was on the political Right, as it is today.

The title of this book indicates that, although in its essential attitudes the party remained the same, its name changed. The word 'Tory', originally an abusive one employed by its opponents, remained as the party label until 1830-2. 'Conservative' gradually crept in, and by the mid-1830s it was well-established. It implied that the party was seeking to broaden its appeal to include all the conservative forces which were opposed to the Whigs. Even after the break-up over the Corn Laws, when Peel's 'new Conservative Party' suffered a devastating set-back, the term was still used, although the young Disraeli did something to bring 'Tory' back into fashion. He was keen to place himself in a long Tory tradition which pre-dated Peel's leadership and which placed a greater emphasis upon the preservation of institutions and of the old social order.

By 1886 it was the Liberals' turn to split (over Home Rule for Ireland), and those who broke away, such as the Radical, Joseph Chamberlain, and the Whig, Lord Hartington, saw themselves as 'Liberal Unionists'. They believed in the union of Britain and Ireland, as brought about in 1800, and shared this attitude with Lord Salisbury and the Conservatives. In time these Liberal Unionists became more closely identified with the Salisbury governments, and some of them served in his final administration, which was a Conservative and Liberal Unionist one. The shorter term 'Unionist' was frequently used by politicians and commentators to describe those who belonged to the conservative cause, although it was not until 1911 that the Liberal Unionists and the Conservatives formally merged, to become the Conservative and Unionist Party of today.

Under whatever label they operated, the Conservatives rested their support primarily upon the landed interest. However, as land lost its overwhelming importance in society with the onward march of industrialism, the party reached out to incorporate those who obtained their wealth from other sources, such as the owners of commercial and industrial undertakings.

The Political Right in Britain between 1815 and 1914

Date	Label	Main Prime Ministers
1815-32	Tory	Lord Liverpool (1815-27)
1832-86	Conservative	Sir Robert Peel (1841-6)
		Benjamin Disraeli (1868, 1874-80)
1886-1914	Conservative	Lord Salisbury (1886-92, 1895-1902)
	& Unionist	Arthur Balfour (1902-5)

3 The Nature of Conservatism

Conservatives have an instinctive preference for society as it is: the very name implies a desire to preserve what already exists. In Britain, this has not meant hostility to all change. Merely to wish to defend the status quo or to put the clock back to some bygone age is not Conservatism - it is blind reaction. The point was well made by Peter Viereck in *Conservatism Revisited.* He stressed that:

1 Not all the past is worth keeping. The conservative conserves discriminately, the reactionary indiscriminately. Though the events of the past are often shameful and bloody, its lessons are indispensable. By 'tradition', the conservative means all the lessons
5 of the past, but only the ethically acceptable events. The reactionary means all the events.

The emphasis is upon preserving the best of the past, for as Burke argued, 'a disposition to preserve and an ability to improve, taken together, would be my standard of a statesman'. For Conservatives there is a preference for continuity. They feel that the onus of proof rests on those who wish to make changes.

Conservative ideas are not easy to summarise, for as Ian Gilmour has written in *Inside Right* (1977), 'so far, then, as philosophy or doctrine is concerned, the wise Conservative travels light'. Conservatives distrust ideology and dogma, and do not believe that society can be improved by making changes based on abstract theories or a preconceived blueprint for action. They distrust plans and detailed programmes and are often said to be pragmatic and empirical in their search for practical solutions to problems. It is perhaps significant that most of the writing about Conservative thought has been done by practising politicians, such as Burke, Disraeli, Lord Hugh Cecil and Ian Gilmour, rather than by political philosophers.

There is no unchanging body of doctrine in Conservatism. Conservatives distrust abstract reasoning, and adjust their policies in the light of experience and circumstances. They are sceptical of any proposal which seems to conflict with human nature, and dislike change for the sake of change. Their approach to change is evolutionary - building upon the foundations of the past whilst adapting to changing conditions. Adaptation has been the key to British Conservatism for, as Disraeli recognised, the Conservatives have never believed in finality. Although some have been more rigid in their thinking than others, most have accepted the need to adjust as time passes. Lord Salisbury, himself no progressive in the Party, once described the commonest political error as 'sticking to the carcasses of dead policies'. Supporters of the Conservative approach would argue that this shedding of obsolete shibboleths has had more to do with realism than with lack of principle.

4 Burkeian Themes

Many strands of thinking have contributed to Conservative thought. The party is a reflection of its past and is 'a river into which many tributaries have flowed'. Yet certain ideas have regularly recurred over the years and have been accepted by Conservatives in every generation - the importance of religion, the desirability of social stability, the rule of law, and the necessity of upholding civil and political liberty. Many of them were expressed by Burke, writing at the time of the French Revolution.

He stressed the importance of religion and the value of its recognition by the state. He saw it as 'the basis of civil society, and the source of all good, and of all comfort'. Many Conservative writers since then have taken the view that men and women, with all their imperfections, can never be made better by legislation. They believe that if those individuals base their behaviour on a religious view of life, then it is more likely that their lives will be enriched and their duties to others fulfilled. In the nineteenth century there was a close link between the Church of England (the Anglican Church) and the Tory Party. The Church was often portrayed as the Tory Party at prayer, and on matters ranging from education to the emancipation of Roman Catholics the maintenance of the supremacy of the Church was seen as important by many supporters.

Burke also disapproved of equality and desired to maintain rank and station. It was fundamental to Tory thinking that society is basically hierarchical, based on class, and requires authoritative leadership in order to maintain stability. The authoritative leadership is provided by the governing class, because the art of government requires exceptional talent. It can be practised successfully only by a few, who are in consequence entitled to wealth and privileges to distinguish them from the rest of society. The governed will accept those who govern them because of their obvious talent for leadership and because of a feeling of deference towards the ruling class. In this way the idea of authoritative leadership, which has its origins in the period before the extension of the franchise, could be later reconciled with the democratic tradition which emerged as a result of mass suffrage. According to this view, the role given to the electorate is a limited and passive one. They do not initiate policy, which comes down from their leaders. Conservatives could 'Trust the People' in the confident expectation that the people would respond by choosing them to rule.

Underlying this approach was a defence of the established order in society, a theme caught well in a verse of the Victorian hymn, *All things bright and beautiful:*

> The rich man in his castle,
> The poor man at his gate.
> God made them high and lowly
> And ordered their estate.

Tories had no intention of changing this balance in society, although the more paternalistic might wish to ensure that those who were 'lowly' could enjoy a decent standard of life.

Burke also strongly supported the institution of private property, and was opposed to any injustice being done to individuals in the course of political and social reform. The desire to avoid injustice was a limiting factor on both parties in the nineteenth century and, as a result, state action was viewed with suspicion. Measures to protect workers had a habit of infringing the rights of factory owners, and this made politicians reluctant to interfere with the workings of *laissez-faire.*

Finally, Burke believed that change must be evolutionary and must be carried out in accordance with the nature of the society. He viewed the state as being organic, in that, in his words, it was 'a partnership not only between those who are living, but between those who are living and those who are dead, and those who are to be born'. His feelings for continuity would be shared by most Conservatives, who wish to see a link between the past, the present and the future. As the twentieth-century poet, T.S. Eliot put it in *Burnt Norton:*

> Time present and time past
> Are both perhaps present in time future
> And time future contained in time past.

Conservatives of every generation would echo Burke's dislike of violent change and would wish to see evolution rather than revolution. 'Ordered change' is a phrase much used by Conservative writers.

5 Adaptation in the Nineteenth Century

Much of what Burke wrote was accepted by his successors in the nineteenth century. They usually stressed the need for change to be accomplished in a peaceful, gradual manner which did not infringe the rights of others. Their thinking lacked rigidity, for it was not doctrinaire. Conservative politicians in office were rarely willing to repudiate all innovation. Canning, a progressive Tory of the 1820s, made the point that those who refuse all improvements because they are innovations often find themselves forced to accept innovations when they have ceased to be improvements. In this spirit, Conservative leaders were to give way on a number of occasions. Sometimes changes were made only grudgingly and acceptance was delayed as long as possible. On other occasions Conservatives initiated change. Even in its most negative period, in the years before the First World War, the party did not quite opt to die in the last ditch.

In the 1830s Peel created a tradition of moderate Conservatism. Although he believed in the importance of established institutions, he placed less emphasis upon traditional Tory values than many in the party would have wished. His fall in 1846 placed the whole movement in jeopardy, and it was his arch-opponent over the Repeal of the Corn Laws, Disraeli, who made the larger input into Tory thinking. He desired to uphold cherished institutions such as the Monarchy and the Church. He also thought in terms of a natural alliance between the aristocracy and the people, and espoused popular principles.

> The Tory party is only in its proper position when it represents popular principles. Then it is truly irresistible. Then it can uphold the throne and the majesty of the empire, the liberty of the nation, and the rights of the multitude.

Many of his ideas have had an influence on the modern party. His Tory Democracy may have been a vague and romantic notion rather than a concrete reality, but he taught the Conservative party that policies serving only the interests of one class could only be justified if they were genuinely designed to serve the national good rather than a sectional interest. He laid claim to a Conservatism which transcended class barriers and was representative of the needs and aspirations of the whole community. It was patriotic abroad and similarly stressed national interests at home.

6 Differing Conceptions of Conservatism

Throughout their histories the Tory and Conservative parties, like most others, have been coalitions made up of people with significantly differing views. The Tory tradition dates back to the predominance of the landed interests which formerly dominated public life and which, at their best, exhibited a decent paternalism in the conduct of affairs. Its members were, on occasion, prepared to use state power to improve living conditions. As the nineteenth century progressed and business interests became more important in the Conservative Party, the commercial and industrial values of the middle classes assumed greater significance. Its representatives stressed the freedom of business men to further their own interests, and shared the *laissez-faire* approach of many

Liberals. They believed that it was not the government's role to regulate economic and social life and were suspicious of state intervention. The Liberal Unionist input of Whigs and the Chamberlainites emphasised those beliefs, stressing the importance of the individual and of individual enterprise. Modern Conservatism still contains exponents of both approaches, Tories and *laissez-faire* liberals, though neither line of argument is normally allowed to dominate party thinking completely.

Donald Southgate, in *The Conservative Leadership: 1832-1932,* has distinguished three viewpoints common to the Conservative approach and has found a quotation from Lord Salisbury to illustrate each one. The 'Diehard view' was expressed in a comment made in 1859: 'Hostility to radicalism, incessant, implacable hostility, is the essential definition of Conservatism'. He sounded a little less uncompromising in 1863, when he spoke of, '[contenting] ourselves with patching a little here, and altering a bit there'. Such a view, Southgate remarks, was couched 'in rigidly defensive terms, but scope is allowed for flexibility and reform'. Shortly before he first became Prime Minister, he sounded more constructive,

> The object of our party is not and ought not to be simply to keep things as they are. In the first place, the enterprise is impossible. In the next place, there is much in our present mode of thought and action, which it is highly undesirable to conserve.

In this comment he placed himself much more in the lineage of Peel and Disraeli, and was a spokesman for moderate and desirable change.

Studying 'Nineteenth-Century Conservatism'

After studying this topic students will not normally be asked questions which survey the position of the Conservative Party during the whole of the nineteenth century. Traditionally the main targets for examiners have been Lord Liverpool - in both his earlier 'repressive' and his later 'reforming' phases - Peel, Disraeli, Salisbury and Balfour. Occasionally other important figures, such as Canning, Lord Randolph Churchill and Joseph Chamberlain, have been the focus of attention. With all of these leading politicians, whilst it is important to understand what they did and why they did it, it is just as important to be able to place them in the context of nineteenth-century Conservatism and show what they contributed to Conservative thought and practice. Sometimes comparison is possible. For example, it is useful to think about the similarities and differences between Peelite and Disraelian Conservatism, and the legacy of each to the modern Conservative Party. You would be well advised to keep both approaches firmly in mind as you work on the rest of this book.

CHAPTER 2

The Origins of the Party

In their attitude to public affairs people tend to fall into two very broad groups: those who are progressive and anxious to promote change and social improvement, and those who emphasise a desire for continuity and are more conservative in their outlook. Those in the second category prefer to let change come about gradually and this instinct for caution in the conduct of business has always been a strong one. Yet, although there has always been a distinctively conservative approach, there was no organised political party to advance such a viewpoint until the nineteenth century. Then, the division into those who promoted and those who were wary of change became the basis of political loyalties.

Before 1800 parties were distinguished more by historical and personal factors than by any distinctive and enduring philosophical differences. The terms 'Whig' and 'Tory' did not stand for particular policies or give any significant clue to the beliefs of those who employed them to describe their approach to politics. Indeed, independence in the House of Commons was an important qualification, which was far more highly rated than allegiance to a particular cause of the moment.

Attempts have been made to trace the origins of political parties back to the seventeenth century - to the time of Charles I. Supporters of one national established Church rather than a series of diverse religious groups and those who backed the king against the Puritans have been seen as early Tories. Those who disliked the idea of one unified Protestant Church and favoured the existence of a number of sects have been labelled as the forerunners of the Whigs. It has been argued that at the time of the Civil War (1642-9) the former rallied to the Royalist cause while the latter opposed it. Whereas the Whigs were attached to religious liberty and to parliament, the Tories stood for Church and king. Keith Feiling, in the first edition of his *History of the Tory Party, 1640-1714*, published in 1924, referred to 'two twin schools of thought ... decisively opposed to each other on the causes which most divide mankind - on religious truth and political power'. Following the work of Sir Lewis Namier in the 1930s, he subsequently modified his position and was uneasy about his use of the word 'party' in the title of his book, although he still claimed that there had been 'a continuous tradition and some elementary framework of party and a descent of political ideas'.

Some historians have taken 1678 as their starting-point for the beginning of political parties. In that year there was a proposal to exclude Charles II's younger brother, James, the Duke of York, from the throne because of his avowed Roman Catholicism. Those who supported his succession were accused of showing a sympathy for the Catholic Church and the term 'Tory' was used to describe them. An abusive reference, it referred to the Catholic outlaws who lived in the middle, 'bog', counties of Ireland - hence the literal meaning of Tory as 'bog-trotters'. Similarly, 'Whig' was an unflattering term for those politicians who supported parliament against the king, who stressed the liberties of the people, and who wanted religious toleration for all except Roman Catholics. The term alludes to the roving brigands of the Western Lowlands of Scotland, the Whiggamores.

In the Glorious Revolution of 1688 James abdicated to be replaced by the Protestant William of Orange from Holland. Both Whigs and Tories favoured the abdication for they had found the Catholic king impossible to work with. But, whereas the Whigs welcomed the subsequent reduction in royal authority and the supremacy of parliament, the Tories were attached to the idea of an hereditary succession to the throne and to the predominance of the Crown. Some historians would claim that after 1688 there remained a clear distinction between Whigs and Tories. Furthermore, whereas Charles II had been able to rule with advisers of different political leanings, this was not so after the Revolution. Monarchs found that a mixed ministry of both groups normally proved unworkable.

1 Tories and Whigs in the Eighteenth Century

There were, then, groups of people who called themselves Tories. But such terminology was loose. For much of the eighteenth century there was little indication of the survival of Feiling's 'First Tory Party', and in the second volume of his work he wrote that it had 'vanished as though it had never been'. The party was a long time actually dying, and, although it lingered for a while, it was deprived of office. Sir Robert Walpole, the Whig statesman and effectively the first British Prime Minister, purged Tories who had served in local and central government. Essentially, there was a non-party basis for most parliamentary activity from the supremacy of Walpole (1721-42) to the arrival on the scene of the Younger Pitt in 1783, and 'party' virtually disappeared in the middle of the century.

There were writers and pamphleteers who called themselves Tories. One of these was Jonathan Swift who was most famous as the author of *Gulliver's Travels*. He portrayed Whigs as politicians who sought to reduce the king's power, extend religious toleration, and protect the monied rather than the landed interest in the community. By contrast, he described a Tory as a firm supporter of the national interest. Tories were those men whose attachment was not to a particular ministry but was to the patriotic cause: men who would 'do their utmost to save their prince and their country, whoever be at the helm'. Swift was anxious to preserve the constitution as by law established. He lamented that parliament had declined into faction, by which he meant groupings of politicians seeking offices of profit from motives of private ambition, status and personal gain.

Not long afterwards Viscount Bolingbroke was repeating similar arguments against party. He had been prominent among the more extreme Tories early in the century, had served in office and, on Queen Anne's death in 1714, had been keen to see the son of James II become king. However, James refused to renounce his Catholicism, Bolingbroke was discredited, and the Hanoverians came to the throne. This led to the Whigs gaining a monopoly of power, and Bolingbroke (not surprisingly in the circumstances) becoming anti-party. Like Swift he felt that there had once been differences over fundamental principles between Whigs and Tories but, in his view, by the 1740s the use of the names merely contributed to the spreading of bitterness and hatred. He wanted men to forget their unreasonable disagreements and unite to achieve a common objective, the happiness of their country - 'Let the very names of Whig and Tory be forever buried in Oblivion'. For Bolingbroke, a free people implied a patriarchal family, united by bonds of common interest and motivated by a common spirit, and he saw the king as the guarantor of the national as opposed to the party interest. Such views were held by many of the country gentlemen of the time - the permanent 'out' politicians, men excluded from power for whatever reason. Perhaps it was only to be expected that those who could not attain office tended to argue that parties and factions were undesirable because they acted as a barrier to good government.

Many contemporaries looked with distrust on any classification of men into two opposing groups, Whigs and Tories, and felt that such divisions had been damaging to the country in the past. In as much as they existed, the distinctions were historical, family, and local ones, rather than the result of conflicts over major issues of policy or principle. To talk of parties is, therefore, potentially misleading, although there were plenty of people who liked to refer to themselves by one or other of the two labels. And they do indicate what Professor Gash has called 'types, temperaments, traditions and connections'. Tories emphasised patriotic values, and support for Church and king.

Dr Johnson, the literary genius of the eighteenth century, was in no doubt about his leanings for he was of the opinion that 'the first Whig was the Devil'. He characterised a Tory as someone 'with an instinctive reverence for what was established, a respect for government and the Crown, a loyalty towards the Church of England and a prejudice in favour of the landed interest'. By contrast, he thought of Whigs as those inclined to innovation, who championed the popular interest (when it suited them to do so), who were jealous of executive power and distrustful of ecclesiastical authority. He was using stereotypes which convey the feel of contemporary modes of thought, but they offer little indication of how people reacted in particular circumstances. Despite his strong preferences he was able to write in 1781, 'A wise Tory and a wise Whig, I believe, will agree [that] ... a High Tory makes government unintelligible [and] ... a violent Whig makes it impracticable'.

For most politicians the over-riding concern was to achieve office and to remain there. Once in power they frequently behaved as their predecessors had done rather than in the way they had reacted when in opposition. In such a fluid situation the Elder Pitt, a Whig who disclaimed party connection, was often supported by Tories during the middle years of the century.

2 Namier's Analysis of Eighteenth-Century Politics

The terms Whig and Tory may have existed in the eighteenth century, there may have been factions or tendencies, but there was nothing like a two-party system as we know it today. Sir Lewis Namier in *Monarchy and the Party System* (1952) claimed that it was misleading to think about the period in these terms, and that parliamentary action was not based on differences of principle and ideas. He felt that labels which related to the reign of Charles II did not provide a useful basis for understanding the differences between politicians in their pursuit of political power. He preferred to divide politicians into three broad groups, believing that this provided a more realistic analysis of parliamentary life.

1 1   There were the followers of the Court and the current administration, who were permanently 'ins' - placemen pledged to support the government of the day as long as it had the confidence of the king.
5 2   On the opposing side were the independent country gentlemen who remained independent by their own choice and were permanently 'outs'. These were mostly representatives from the shires and they gave any government appointed by the king an opportunity to prove itself. They saw themselves as guardians of
10 the national interest and were not interested in participating in power. They held aloof and prided themselves on their incorruptibility.
3   In between was the group of professional politicians, such as Walpole and the Pitts, who sought office and struggled for power.
15 Such people were the early exponents of modern parliamentary practice. They were men whose concern was to ensure that they were returned to the House with as many of their supporters as possible.

Namier's analysis is a useful one but even this classification gives little indication of the complex web of cliques and factions which dominated the House of Commons until well into the following century. The shifting loyalties of a group of MPs who were relatives or who sat for neighbouring constituencies could easily bring about the fall of any government.

For Frank O'Gorman, in *The Emergence of the British Two-Party*

System, 1760-1832 (1982), there did still remain a Tory tradition which lingered throughout the period, but 'This is not ... to argue that the Tory party in any sense survived as a coherent body'. He identifies the willingness of the bulk of Tory country gentlemen to support the Court as a distinguishing feature, and notes that by the 1770s there was developing a conservative alliance between Crown, the government and the gentry. The issue which brought this about was the struggle of the American colonies for independence from Great Britain, an issue on which these groups supported a policy of coercion to put down the American rebellion. O'Gorman sees this as the beginnings of the 'conservative reaction' which is more usually dated from the French Revolution of 1789.

3 Edmund Burke

Edmund Burke was originally a prominent Whig, although he was to go down in history as the father of modern Conservative thinking. His *Thoughts on the Cause of the Present Discontents* (1770) offered a defence of party as a regular and useful element in political life. He saw the association of like-minded men as a natural phenomenon of political activity. He argued that, although they would inevitably differ in their opinions about how they should reach their long-term goals, they could achieve more of them by acting together to promote their common interests and ideas than through independent action. Whereas others saw parties as at best divisive and at worst unpatriotic, he saw them as the means by which men's beliefs could be given clear political expression. In his apologia for party he argued that parties should be founded on 'great leading general principles in government'. Members would generally be in accord with each other, although he did not want them to blindly follow those in charge when their behaviour conflicted with their own convictions.

He was not describing the political scene which then existed, and was aware that his theories were unacceptable to many contemporaries. He pointed the way forward but until the next century there was still a general suspicion of party which was equated in many people's minds with conspiracy and factionalism. For the same reason the idea of an official opposition in the House of Commons did not attract any widespread support.

4 The French Revolution

The pattern of political behaviour was disturbed by the French Revolution which sparked off a fundamental debate about the manner and pace of change in society, and in so doing fractured the alignment of party groups. Opinions cut across traditional ties, and in Britain former friends and partners found themselves at loggerheads. At first some people welcomed the upheaval in France as a liberation. They saw it as the dawn of liberty in a country long oppressed by Bourbon rule, and hoped that it might lead to the development of a constitutional monarchy. From the beginning others were suspicious of what was happening.

Burke was not convinced that the circumstances of such a revolt could yield a beneficial outcome. He wrote his *Reflections on the Revolution in France* in November 1790, after the fall of the Bastille, but before the imprisonment and eventual execution of Louis XVI, the outbreak of war, and the Reign of Terror. He had long supported ancient liberties and rights but he did not see the Revolution as a means of protecting them. He saw no genuine comparison with England in 1688 and believed that the apparently liberal beliefs of the early French revolutionaries would be exploited by others who did not share any commitment to liberty. The outcome would be at best weakness and anarchy, at worst bloodshed and tyranny. He dismissed the theorists of revolution as naive in their optimism of a better future, and claimed that 'In the groves of their academy, at the end of every vista you can see the gallows'.

He stressed the need for an ordered society 'to liberate the best elements in mankind, and restrain the worst'. Society must develop naturally as an organic entity with its own character and at its own pace. There was an important place for religion and morality. Rulers ought to rule with restraint as they maintained social order, whilst the governed needed to accept certain basic values which made possible a civilised existence. In this way, the social fabric of a country could be preserved.

Despite his reverence for the past, its social structure and institutions, Burke was not a blind reactionary. He regarded some change as necessary. His previous record had shown a dislike of cruelty, and on issues such as slavery, the rights of Catholics and independence for the American colonies there was an enlightened strain in his thinking. He argued that the maintenance of the status quo must never become so rigid that change could not occur, for as he remarked, 'a state without the means of some change is without the means of its conservation'.

Although he recognised that an unwillingness even to contemplate change could provoke just the violent upheaval in society of which he so despaired, he was very uneasy about any democratic stirrings at home and was alarmed by signs of discontent in the industrial areas where radical opinion was becoming more organised. His wish to see the nation rally to fend off such radical subversion was widely shared. Many people of conservative persuasion feared that there was a serious threat to the landed classes in particular, and more generally to the whole existing social order. Burke's writings gave classic expression to their fears. They also liked his emphasis upon the importance of the Church in society, for some of them had noticed an anti-religious drift in France as the Revolution unfolded. For these reasons he became a popular figure among the aristocrats who had shunned him for years. The occasional extravagance of his language had led some to regard him as suspect in his judgement of issues, but this time his views seemed to be vindicated by events. Many people were shocked at the speed with which the Revolution entered an aggressive phase, with violence and cruelty quickly followed by dictatorship.

A section among the Whigs lost any initial enthusiasm for the events of 1789 once the French monarchy fell and the Revolutionaries talked of aiding revolution everywhere. The threat to the hereditary principle and to the rights of property in Britain caused them alarm, and some of them crossed the floor of the Commons in 1794. Hating what he heard from France, Burke went with them and joined the coalition led by the Younger Pitt in the hope of helping the country to weather the storm, for since 1793 Britain and France had been at war. After leaving the Whigs Burke became more opposed to political and social change, for he was appalled by the extreme radicalism of the Jacobin faction then ruling France. In a comment which reflects his new political allegiance he spoke in 1796 of 'the cackling of us poor Tory geese' as he issued warnings about the need for stronger national defence. By then, a year before his death in 1797, he was suggesting that one-fifth of the British people had pro-Jacobin sympathies.

Burke provided the first explicit analysis of Conservatism and he is often seen as the founding-father of the modern creed. His observations are of enduring value and the *Reflections* have become a seminal text for those who wish to delve into right-wing political thinking. Expressed in fine literary style and highly quotable, the work, in Norman Gash's words, 'outlived his age, because it was based not simply on the historical circumstances of his time but on a profound insight into the nature of man in society'.

After Burke and some other Whigs had joined with the supporters of the Younger Pitt, accepting office or pledging support in the House of Commons, British political life was characterised by a cautious conservatism in the conduct of affairs. The Whigs shrunk to a solidly Foxite element - named after their leader, Charles James Fox, who had welcomed the Revolution as the dawn of liberty in France. He saw it as a replica of the Glorious Revolution of 1688 and, although he was later shocked by some of its savagery, he clung to his belief that the cause of reform across the Channel was the cause of progress everywhere. His long friendship with Burke was broken by their difference of views and he dissolved into tears when they parted ways in 1794.

5 William Pitt

In entering into war with France Pitt had no ideological end in view, whereas Burke was concerned to extinguish the flame of revolution in order to stop it spreading further afield. Although Pitt later rallied the country using rhetoric which echoed Burke's sentiments and spoke of 'the liquid fire of Jacobinical principles destroying the world', his motives were more practical. In his view, Britain was fighting primarily to defend its commercial and colonial interests.

Pitt had been Prime Minister since December 1783 when he was 24. At the time he took office, Fox mocked him as a schoolboy head of a 'mincepie administration', doomed to end as soon as the seasonal mincepies were consumed - yet he remained as Premier until 1801. His career was his life. He never married and he devoted all his time and energy to serving the nation. He brought exceptional gifts of character to the task. More of an administrator than a politician, he was intelligent, industrious, pragmatic, patient and determined. In the House of Commons he was a skilful orator in an age of great debaters, and he established a towering ascendancy. He also had a reputation for aloofness and inaccessibility.

When he first became Prime Minister he could not always be sure of securing full backing for his policies, for Cabinet members often differed in their opinions. But he was the man whose views mattered, and he established a pre-eminence over his colleagues. Popular in the country and well-regarded in the commercial world, he dominated British political life much as Sir Robert Peel was to do a generation later, and there was no real rival as an acceptable head of the government. Under his leadership the position of Prime Minister developed in significance for he believed that,

1 There should be an avowed and real minister possessing the chief weight in council and the principal place in the confidence of the king. In that respect, there can be no rivalry or division of power. That power must rest with the person generally called the First 5 Minister.

He tried to co-ordinate the policy of the government to give it a clear sense of direction, and he accustomed people to the idea of administrative and financial competence. He set an example of personal honour and integrity, and within the public service showed zeal in seeking high standards of behaviour and good value for money. William Huskisson, later himself to be a senior Cabinet Minister in the early nineteenth century, observed that 'everything that drops from him is ... marked by superior virtue and superior sense'. Huskisson and others of the generation were to become protegés of Pitt, but the Prime Minister was never a strong party figure and had only a small band of personal followers.

He had initially had some sympathy with the moderate French revolutionaries and had hoped that France 'would soon enjoy just that kind of liberty which I venerate'. But he became alarmed as that country lapsed into a cycle of terror and aggression. He hoped to avoid war, but an active French foreign policy meant that the impact of the Revolution was spreading into Europe. Pitt was troubled by the possible threat to British interests and European order, and his anxiety was widely shared.

France declared war on Britain in February 1793 and Pitt had the support to make him the obvious war leader. He tried to unite the country in its patriotic endeavour, and had the rhetorical gifts necessary to inspire the nation, if not the tactical grasp of warfare. Inevitably, he was in the position of reacting to events across the Channel, and in doing so he showed himself to be a superior statesman to many of his European contemporaries.

The mood of the House of Commons was generally conservative, but in the country at large there had for some time been indications of a growing political consciousness. Radicals had agitated against bad government, electoral corruption, and the excessive influence of the Crown. They felt that reform was necessary in order to restore a sound constitution. Hopes of political reform had been dashed when Pitt himself had tried and failed to carry resolutions for moderate parliamentary reform through the House in 1785.

By the 1790s there were a number of Radical societies. Some were aristocratic in tone and were linked with the Foxite group in the Commons. Others were made up of artisans who wanted wholesale reform of the parliamentary system. When some used the French style of address and the language of the Revolution it created alarm among the governing classes who saw them as condoning the violence in France. One of the Radical heroes was Tom Paine, who in 1791-2 wrote his book *The Rights of Man* which was a justification of the French Revolution. He personally disliked mob rule, as did many of his supporters, but they were all denounced as 'Jacobins'. In the 1790s the Pitt government turned to repression to crush the societies and this drove popular agitation underground, although it continued to burst forth from time to time. Paine was prosecuted for seditious libel, and *habeas corpus* (the right of every detained person to be brought to trial) was suspended, amid other measures to stamp out disorder. In 1799-1800, the Combination Acts, outlawing trade unions because they were thought to be another source of possible sedition, were passed.

In 1802 a temporary peace between Britain and France was signed, but by then Pitt was no longer in power. He had wrestled with the problems of Ireland and wanted a just settlement of issues affecting her. He favoured and brought about the Union of Great Britain and Ireland in 1800 but believed that it needed to be followed by other measures of pacification. He supported Catholic Emancipation, the right of Catholics to be able to sit in the House of Commons and to hold public office. Many of his colleagues did not support him this time, and George III was resolute in his opposition. The Prime Minister misjudged the king's reaction and when Pitt offered his resignation in 1801, it was accepted.

However, he was in power again between 1804 and 1806. But this was a troubled period and his administration was less successful than his first one had been. He was not to see the end of the war, for he died in 1806, an exhausted man and still only 46 years old. He had come to symbolise the nation's effort and he left behind him a devoted band of admirers who wished to perpetuate his memory.

Chris Patten, a modern Conservative politician and writer on *The Tory Case* has detected three strands of thought in the era of Burke, Pitt and the French Revolution - strands which remain an essential part of the party's approach today.

1 First, there was opposition to systems, to political blue-prints and to utopianism; this went hand-in-hand with a profound scepticism about the rationalist approach to life. Secondly, there was a defence of property and order, and an organic view of society.
5 Thirdly, there was an unashamed patriotism, a defence of Crown and of country, and of the British national interest.

Pitt was not the leader of a well-organised party, with a majority in the House of Commons. He was not the people's choice, but that of the king, and he stayed in office for as long as he did because he generally enjoyed royal support. He had a small band of fifty or sixty personal followers, although he and his ministers could usually count on many more who were willing to support anyone who enjoyed Crown backing.

Moreover, although many writers place Pitt in the Tory tradition, others are uneasy because of one major problem. He was not a Tory, and he never called himself one. He was an independently-minded Whig who saw himself as part of a great Whig tradition going back to 1688. Above all, he was not a party politician. He believed that governments should be formed from the best available talent. However, because of his obvious political skills and his approach to public affairs, Conservative writers like to include him in the gallery of their famous predecessors. This is not unreasonable because his attitudes were fundamentally conservative, and his desire for moderate reform accompanied by social discipline among the 'lower orders' at a time of radical unrest, identifies him as a firm supporter of that 'ordered liberty' of which Conservatives are apt to speak.

The development of the French Revolution and the growth of radicalism at home helped to polarise opinion between reformer and conservative. On the one hand were those such as Fox who stood for constitutional liberty and progress, and who called themselves Whigs. On the other were those who wished to resist the popular tide and defend the constitution as it was. The second group included landowners and many of the professional and business classes, some of whom were in the process of becoming landowners, as well as the bulk of the clergy. It was reinforced by the 'old Whigs' as Burke sometimes called them, who shared conservative values. It is from this Pittite coalition of forces that something which can be distinguished as Toryism emerged.

6 The Development of Toryism, 1806-11

After Pitt's death a 'Ministry of the Talents' took over. But it did not include the Pittites whose main standard-bearers were George Canning and William Huskisson. They dreamed of one day recreating the old Pitt ministry in the spirit of their dead hero. Meanwhile, they met regularly for political dinners and committed themselves to broad support for the government as long as Pitt's policies were not abandoned. When they detected 'backsliding' they became vigorous in opposition, although with limited success because they lacked leadership and were but one of a number of parliamentary groups. George III replaced the 'Talents' ministry and in the general election which followed soon afterwards, in 1807, those who supported his action, mainly the Pittites, used the label 'Tory' and those who opposed it called themselves 'Whigs'.

Over the next few years the memory of Pitt faded and what held his followers together was no longer just his legacy but also a common attachment to upholding the king's policies and position. Spencer Perceval, Prime Minister between 1809 and 1812, pinpointed this transformation from 'Pittism' to Toryism in his observation that,

> The magic of that [Pitt's] name is in a great degree dissolved, and the principle upon which we must rely to keep us together, and to give us the assistance of floating strength, is the public sentiment of loyalty and attachment to the king.

Following the fall of Pitt's main ministry in 1801 there was a succession of six Prime Ministers in less than 12 years. However, there was considerable continuity in policy for much of the time, and a nucleus of senior ministers was often in office. They stood for the vigorous prosecution of the war against France, discouragement of the radical reform movement at home, an end to discussion of the Catholic question for the time being, and a general responsiveness to the wishes of the monarch.

7 The Beginning of the Liverpool Era

In 1812, after a period of parliamentary confusion, Lord Liverpool took office and formed an administration which was to remain in power for 15 years. Its members and policies were labelled by their opponents as Tory even if the term was not one that Liverpool would have chosen to employ. It was a Tory ministry because it upheld just the sort of attitudes that Pitt had represented in the 1790s and which had become widely accepted platitudes by 1812 - namely loyalty to Church and king, the maintenance of law and order at home, and defence of the nation's security from external threat. As the Opposition was happy to be thought of as 'Whig' it was natural that the government should be seen as 'Tory' whether or not it approved of the use of the label. Furthermore, although Liverpool still thought of himself as primarily a servant of the king rather than as a party spokesman, unlike Pitt he was willing to organise a parliamentary following for his government.

For Liverpool, Burke was the greatest philosopher and Pitt the greatest statesman who had ever lived. Since the day that Burke crossed the floor and supported the Pittite coalition there has been, in Blake's words, a 'continuous and definable Tory tradition'. As he observed, the attitudes of a person who was a Tory near the beginning of the nineteenth century would have been recognisable to his counterpart today.

Making notes on 'The Origins of the Party'

This chapter clearly fits into the category of 'background' to a study of politics in nineteenth-century Britain. After reading it you should understand the contribution made by writers and thinkers in the eighteenth century to the origins of the Conservative Party. You should also be aware of how the nineteenth-century Tory Party was based on the legacy of Pitt the Younger. The notes you make should be very brief and should be compiled primarily to ensure that these general understandings have been acquired. It may be sufficient merely to copy the summary diagram for the chapter.

Origins in the late seventeenth century
|

Not an effective parliamentary grouping   key figures
in the eighteenth century   Swift (emphasis on patriotic cause)
                                       Bolingbroke (similar emphasis on
| national, not party, interests)
                                       Burke (horror of violent change
1783 William Pitt the Younger   in France reflected fear of
(Independent Whig) became PM   conservative element in society)

|

1793 Pittite coalition fought war with France   outlook
| patriotic; conservative in its
                                       opposition to radicalism at home
1806 Death of Pitt
| outlook
Emergence of Pittite Lord Liverpool as PM   • church and king Toryism
| • maintenance of *status quo*
1815 Defeat of Napoleon. Liverpool still PM • preservation of landed interest
                                             • opposition to political radicalism

Summary - The Origins of the Party

CHAPTER 3

The Tories, 1815-32

1 Introduction

When Lord Liverpool became Prime Minister in 1812 he was not expected to survive in office for very long. In its early months his government seemed so insecure that it looked as though it would barely outlive its infancy. However, he was fortunate that this period coincided with a revival of Britain's fortunes in the wars against the French, for many people were pleased by Wellington's victories and this made them contented with the government's general handling of affairs. After the return of peace in 1815 the country was beset with problems, but having overcome the early difficulties, Liverpool contrived to remain in office until 1827, and his party continued to do so for three years longer.

The Tories were also fortunate to be faced by opponents who for much of the time were weak, ineffectual and lacking in strong leadership. The breakaway of some Whigs to join the Pittite coalition in 1794 had seriously demoralised their former party, and for many years it was unable to offer sustained opposition. Divisions within the Whigs' ranks made it easier for the Tory government to fend off defeat in the House of Commons for, although many MPs could not be relied on to back Lord Liverpool and his colleagues, they were even less disposed to see them overthrown and the Whigs installed in their place. The voters, who made up only 2 per cent of the population, agreed, and the elections of 1818 and 1826 confirmed the government's dominant parliamentary position.

In the years immediately after the end of the Napoleonic Wars in 1815 the policy of the government was based on fear. Leaders recalled the revolutionary upheavals in France and were shocked when they heard reports of inflammatory speeches by British radicals who were agitating for parliamentary reform. It seemed all too reminiscent of the excesses of the French Revolution. In these circumstances the government did little more than defend the status quo. It placed more emphasis on a firm approach to maintaining law and order than on a policy of redressing real grievances.

In the early 1820s, as the memory of the Revolution grew dimmer in people's minds, the new and younger ministers were to be responsible for constructive change, for they realised that to accept cautious innovation did not necessarily undermine their position. Indeed, they understood that opposing it could have far more dangerous consequences.

After Lord Liverpool's death in 1827 the divisions within the party between moderate reformers and those High Tories on the Right (the Ultras) who opposed almost any concession came to the surface and could not be easily contained. Liverpool's successors lacked his mediating skill, and were unable to unite their colleagues and keep the party together. After the election of 1830, which had been caused by the death of George IV, the government was defeated on a motion supporting the need to change the composition of the House of Commons. Now the Tories were out of office, and in the next two years, under the Duke of Wellington's leadership, they set themselves firmly against parliamentary reform. Despite Tory opposition, the Whigs finally secured the passage of the Great Reform Bill in 1832. In the election which followed, the new electorate inflicted upon the Tories the most decisive defeat in the party's history.

2 Personalities and Policies

The government which Lord Liverpool had formed in 1812 and which had triumphed against Napoleon continued in office after 1815. It contained several members of the old Pittite coalition, notably Lords Eldon, Sidmouth and Castlereagh, as well as the Prime Minister himself. They were joined by younger Tories such as Huskisson, Palmerston and Peel. These men were much influenced by what had happened in France since 1789, where a king and queen had been executed, the nobility decimated, and the whole traditional pattern of life shattered.

a) Lord Liverpool and his Cabinet

An examination of the cabinet of Lord Liverpool, its personnel and their approach, provides a useful insight into the nature of early-nineteenth century Toryism. Historians have not usually written sympathetically of the Prime Minister himself, yet he achieved the feat of surviving as Premier for a longer uninterrupted period than any other leader of the party. It has to be admitted that this was partly due to the lack of a credible alternative for much of the time, but it was also a tribute to his own skill and leadership. His ministry both overcame the initial difficulties it confronted and adjusted itself to the improving conditions of the 1820s.

Lord Liverpool had entered the House in 1790 as Philip Jenkinson and had been elevated to the peerage on his father's death in 1808. He had undergone a long apprenticeship before he reached the top, serving in many ministerial offices. He had not been marked out as possessing obvious prime ministerial potential, and there were others around him of more outstanding ability. He was not intellectually gifted, was not an original thinker, and had a narrow, unimaginative mind. One French observer noted rather unkindly that if he had been present on the day of creation he would have begged God to preserve chaos! His speeches did not inspire and he was wary of change. Disraeli later recognised some of the flaws in his political make-up when he referred to him in *Coningsby* as an 'arch-mediocrity'.

Yet this is not the whole picture for he had useful qualities. His amiable character was much praised by those who knew him well and they recognised his fairness, integrity and dependability. His colleagues liked and trusted him and responded to the free hand he gave them. They could count on his common sense, loyalty and support, and he was able to draw the best out of them. He was also an effective chairman of the Cabinet. By his understated manner he was able to reconcile ministers of widely differing views and maintain harmony. He was not too closely identified with any particular faction and therefore did not antagonise any group. In negotiations he was tactful and he steered a steady and skilful course, making few enemies and winning numerous friends. This emollient style of leadership served the government and party well for many years.

Some of the ministers Lord Liverpool appointed were unimpressive. The Chancellor of the Exchequer, Vansittart, lacked any real grasp of his subject. Lord Sidmouth, the Home Secretary between 1812 and 1822, also did not measure up to the demands of the position. Like his colleagues he was unsure how to tackle the post-war unrest, but his attempts to maintain order were clumsy and were widely thought to be unnecessarily repressive. Deeply conservative, he was later to make his last public speech against Catholic Emancipation and to cast his final vote against the 1832 Reform Bill. Lord Eldon, the long-serving Lord Chancellor, helped Sidmouth draw up much of his restrictive legislation, and was a Tory cast in a similar mould. He opposed any modification of the severe criminal code and resisted Catholic Emancipation and other reform proposals. His approach was unyielding and he could not imagine that the constitutional arrangements of the country could be improved.

However, it was Lord Castlereagh who attracted the greatest public odium. This was despite the fact that he was less unbending in his approach and on Irish and economic affairs was relatively forward-looking. In his early days he had even been attracted by some of the ideas of the French revolutionaries. As well as being Foreign Secretary he was Leader of the House of Commons (of which he was allowed to be a member because he was an Irish peer), and he soon gained a reputation as a 'hard-liner'. Because most of his cabinet colleagues were in the House of Lords it was his task to 'sell' the government's unpopular policies in the House of Commons. His awkward and disdainful manner, perhaps born of shyness, made him ill-fitted for the task and he often mixed his metaphors and became tongue-tied under pressure. He was viciously lampooned by poets and satirists of the day, and it was the poet Shelley who highlighted his cold reserve in the memorable lines of his *Mask of Anarchy;*

I met murder on the way
He had a mask like Castlereagh.

Most members of the Cabinet did not belong to the old aristocracy. In several cases their fathers had been professional men or merchants who had made enough money to buy themselves into the landlord class. They were not all hugely rich, but several gave the impression that they were remote and out of touch with the country. Given their backgrounds and outlook, they were easily ruffled by stories of disorder and unrest.

b) Toryism in 1815

The attitudes of the government are often described as traditional 'Church and King Toryism'. Ministers defended the Anglican Church as one of the great institutions of the state and wished to preserve its privileged position as the established church. They tended to be more hostile towards other denominations than were the Whigs: for instance, they resisted granting full political rights to both Catholics and non-conformists. Concerning the monarchy - even though in 1820 the Prime Minister was to be in sharp disagreement with the new king at the time of the scandal over his private life - they always supported the preservation of royal authority at its current level. Tories were concerned to preserve order and stability, and in the pursuit of this they laid more emphasis on the rights of property than on the rights of individuals. They stressed the importance of land, rather than commerce or industry, as the main form of property, and saw the landed interest as an essential bastion of society. They wished to protect it at all costs.

Drawing their support from those who wished to maintain the status quo, they opposed political reform and were highly sensitive to any radical protest. The political system served them well, and self-interest made them unwilling to entertain any significant change in it. They did not totally oppose all humanitarian reform but most members were reluctant to make any concessions at a time when there was evident lawlessness in the country at large. The trouble was that, although they wished to keep things broadly as they were, the country was in a state of transition and upheaval and many people wanted change and reform.

c) Post-war Distress

In 1815 the country was beset by social and economic difficulties as it moved from war to peace. The fortunes of agriculture and industry were affected by a depression in which unemployment and under-employment (short-time working) sharply increased. The situation was worsened by the rapid increase in population, which was to be characteristic of nineteenth-century Britain as a whole, and the speedy demobilisation of troops at the end of the war, both of which meant that there were even more people looking for work. This was happening against the background of a country which was changing from a predominantly agricultural to a predominantly industrial one, with urban conditions deteriorating as the expansion of factory towns outpaced the provision of services such as sanitation and piped water. For many people the result was that these were times of hardship and gloom.

Government action aggravated the situation. The Corn Laws which it passed in 1815 with Whig support were designed to help the agricultural community by banning the import of corn until domestic prices became very high. Those who owned factories and worked in commerce saw this agricultural protection as a likely impediment to their attempts to export goods, for if Britain would not allow in foreign corn foreigners might be unwilling to accept our manufactured products. Radicals criticised the laws' likely effects on living standards. It was believed that they would keep the price of corn, and therefore of bread, artificially high. Lord Blake, a historian of Conservative sympathies, has described the laws as 'one of the most naked pieces of class legislation in English history'.

Parliament made another move which benefited its own members and further attacked the living standards of the majority of the population when in 1816 it voted to end the Property (or Income) Tax which Pitt had introduced as a wartime expedient. Liverpool and Vansittart saw the continuation of the tax as necessary but they were overruled by the House, which illustrates the difficulty that the government could face in obtaining a Commons majority. To make up the deficiency in government income ministers had to raise indirect taxes on purchases. This disproportionately hit the less-well-off sections of the community.

Those of radical persuasion believed that members of parliament were looking after their own interests and were unable or unwilling to relieve the suffering around the country. In the hope of changing this situation they campaigned to make the House of Commons more representative of the population as a whole. They saw that the existing, unreformed system with its narrow franchise, rotten and pocket boroughs where at most a few people possessed the right to choose the MPs, and open voting resulted in a chamber in which power was primarily in the hands of the landed interest. They thought that only by having a parliament which reflected all or most sections of the community could justice be done and economic grievances tackled.

Parliamentary reform became a regular demand in the speeches of radical agitators. However, the discontent around the country between 1815 and 1820 was not based on one issue alone. It arose out of diverse grievances which varied from locality to locality. Bad harvests, high prices for essential goods, unemployment, poor living conditions and the Corn Laws were common complaints which contributed to the growing mood of protest. Whatever the causes, few doubted the widespread extent of the distress and suffering in both agricultural and in industrial areas. Distress provoked feelings of discontent, and at meetings and marches up and down the country the hungry and unemployed gathered to hear radical orators demand reform. Some demonstrations were peaceful, but at others there was considerable violence.

Strikes, marches and petitions often passed off without serious incident, but there were exceptions. In East Anglia, agricultural labourers carried banners inscribed with the message 'Bread and Blood', and rioting was frequent. In industrial towns in the Midlands and North, factory machinery was smashed. Particularly alarming for Ministers was the gathering at Spa Fields in December 1816, which got out of control; a mob of demonstrators marched towards the City of London, raiding armourer's shops en route. Such agitation terrorised the propertied classes, and restrictive measures were almost inevitable.

In 1817 the Home Secretary decided to act. He suspended *Habeas Corpus*, the legal process which prevented any person from being held in prison without trial, and introduced what became known as the Gagging Acts. Among other things, these clamped down on the holding of seditious meetings. Arrests of prominent agitators, transportation, and execution were part of the government's tough response to the widespread agitation, and Sidmouth employed informers and *agents-provocateurs* to find out about future mass protests. These measures - and better harvests - helped to make the rest of the year and 1818 a more tranquil period, but in 1819 tension returned. At St Peter's Field in Manchester anxious magistrates sent the cavalry into the vast, but orderly, crowd which had gathered to hear 'Orator' Hunt, a Radical MP. In the panic which resulted, 11 people were killed and more than 400 were injured. The disaster (popularly known as Peterloo, a parody of Waterloo, the battle at which Napoleon had been defeated four years previously) aroused public indignation which was only worsened by the government's support for the Manchester magistrates.

The government then passed the Six Acts, a series of measures which seemed very repressive at the time even if they seem less so today. But they were more severe than anything seen up to that time, and among other things they prohibited unauthorised persons from engaging in military exercises, authorised magistrates to issue warrants for searches for arms, and restricted the size of public meetings.

The government had shown itself willing to stamp out disorder. Its firm action against lawlessness, real or imagined, was not matched by measures to alleviate the distress which brought it about. There were some minor reforms, such as the partial abolition of the pillory in 1816, the abolition of the whipping of women in 1820, and, in the previous year, a largely ineffective Factory Act which attempted to place restrictions on child labour. However, such measures provided no solution to the genuine sufferings of hundreds of thousands of people throughout the country.

d) The Tory Response to Disorder

The government thought of the hardship and misery as being inevitable at a time of social and economic change at the end of a long war. They saw such problems as a feature of the natural working of economic laws and felt that there was nothing they could do to lessen the distress. When Lord Liverpool received a proposal to help commercial undertakings in distressed areas his response reflected this view: 'I am satisfied that government or parliament never meddle with these matters at all but they do harm, more or less'. He often quoted the words of a couplet written by Dr Johnson in the eighteenth century.

> How small of all the ills that men endure
> The part which Kings or State can cause or cure.

The Home Secretary felt similarly helpless. In his response to a letter asking for some relief for the suffering peoples of Nottinghamshire, he observed: 'I am concerned to think that the prevailing distress is so severely felt in your county, but I see no reason for believing that it would be alleviated by any proceedings at a public meeting or by parliament itself'.

The experience of Birmingham is an instructive one. Distress there was acute, and in 1819 it was estimated that about 27,000 people were 'on relief'. There was a deep-seated loathing of the Corn Laws and the middle and working classes clamoured for parliamentary reform - after all, Birmingham was not separately represented in the House of Commons. In 1818 the distressed artisans sent parliament a piteous plea for help.

1 We, the undersigned, inhabitants of the town of Birmingham, beg leave ... to inform you of our forlorn and miserable condition ... We are in distress, and in our misery we call upon our country for relief ... We ask no more than your honourable House will acknowledge
5 that good citizens have a right to expect. We ask no favour. We only ask to have it placed within our power to earn honest bread by honest labour. We only ask to be permitted to give our country the benefit of our labour, and receive in exchange the scanty comforts necessary for the support of life. Our wants are only food and
10 clothing, and shelter from the elements ... Many of us have not had any kind of employment for many months, and few of us more than two or three day's work per week, at reduced wages ... A general calamity has fallen upon the whole nation, and has crushed the happiness of all ... we implore your honourable House to remove

15 the cause of misery, whatever it may be. And we cannot but think
that your honourable House can remove it. Or if its roots are so
deeply hidden that no human wisdom can discover them, we must
then consider them as a visitation from Almighty God, to which we
must dutifully bend ... we cannot but think that these calamities
20 originate in natural causes, which it is in the power of human
wisdom to discover and remove ... We humbly pray that your
honourable House will take into consideration our distressed
condition, and adopt such measures as in your wisdom may be
deemed necessary for the relief of ourselves and our suffering
25 country.

The petition seems to have awakened some sympathy within the
government. The Chancellor announced that £1m was to be made
available for the relief of the poor, to be lent to parish authorities and to
be repayable within three years. This illustrates that ministers were not
indifferent to the suffering, but they had little idea of what to do about it.
Neither did many other people - be they politicians, economists or
writers - understand the forces at work. Parliament was lacking in
accurate information about the nature and extent of distress, despite the
special pleading it heard from groups such as the Birmingham citizenry.
Yet even if more had been known, the prevailing philosophy of the day
did not embrace the idea of state action to bring about any
improvement.

The government had no answer to distress, but they were clear in
their own minds that tension was being exacerbated by Radical orators
who exploited the grievances that existed. They suspected that demands
for reform would lead to a revolutionary situation, and when they heard
tales of the use of occasional tricolours and other emblems of the French
Revolutionaries it only confirmed their worst fears. The language of
some of the leaders of popular opinion did suggest that there was reason
to be alarmed. James Ings, one of the Cato Street conspirators who
aimed to assassinate the Cabinet in 1820, explained his intentions in this
way:

1 I will enter the room first. I will go in with a brace of pistols and a
knife in my pocket. After the two swordsmen have despatched
them, I will cut every head off that is in the room, and Lord
Castlereagh's head and Lord Sidmouth's, I will bring away in a
5 bag. For this purpose, I will provide two bags.

Such remarks came only from the wilder fringes of the protesters but
they did seem to confirm the Tory analysis. Ministers believed that a
radical press and seditious leaders were whipping up the feelings of a
'deluded' people and inciting them to insurrection. They did not think
that the mass of people were sufficiently dissatisfied to take action,

unless politically-motivated agitators were arousing them to protest.
They equated any expression of discontent with a threat of revolution
and felt that, if Britain was not to go the way that France had gone after
1789 and the whole fabric of society be ruined, strict law and order must
be maintained.

The dangers were often much exaggerated and, despite the
widespread frustration and alarm, there was little likelihood that Britain
would follow the French experience. But demands for reform, when
accompanied by any signs of widespread organisation and the threat of
violence, made ministers unwilling to take the risk. The government was
fearful and uncomprehending, but was not as sinister or as blindly
repressive as radical publicists of the day often claimed. The verdict of
the Hammonds, two early twentieth-century historians, overstated the
extent of its dictatorial nature: 'Probably no English government has
ever been quite so near, in spirit and licence, to the atmosphere that we
used to associate with the Tsar's government of Russia'.

In its desire to uphold the traditional way of life of the propertied
classes, the government could fairly be charged with self-interest. But in
this, of course, they echoed the feelings of the propertied classes
throughout the country. In the Pitt Clubs set up to honour 'the pilot who
weathered the storm', feelings ran high against 'malicious' and
'dangerous' extremists, and talk of underground conspiracies was rife.
Whigs as well as Tories were alarmed, and Lord Grey on the Whig side
was also fearful that the situation would get out of hand. Of the popular
leaders he asked, 'Is there one of them with whom you would trust
yourself in the dark?'.

Lacking a police force and ultimately reliant on the troops, the
government naturally backed the unpaid local magistrates who had the
responsibility for maintaining order. Normally members of the landlord
class or the clergy, these men feared that the established order was in
danger. Ministers felt it was their duty to support them in public,
whatever their private doubts. As Canning put it after Peterloo, 'To let
down the magistrates would be to invite their resignation and to lose all
gratuitous service in the counties liable to distress for ever'.

e) Economic Toryism

In its economic policy Liverpool's government found itself in
disagreement with both the landed and the business classes at different
times. The economic situation was central to the post-war difficulties for
the problems were of unprecedented severity. The years after Waterloo
were bound to be difficult transitional ones as the restoration of peace
meant that industries which had flourished in the war found their goods
no longer in great demand. At first, the government seemed more
sensitive to the position of the landed interest, and the Corn Laws
showed the importance they attached to the position of agriculture in the

community. Boyd Hilton, in *The Economic Policies of the Tory Government, 1815-30*, has shown that ministers were anxious to ensure food supplies and full employment and saw agriculture as the sector most likely to bring these about. Other interests viewed the 1815 laws very differently.

The loss of the anticipated revenue from the Income Tax was a serious blow to national finances and the government found itself with a shortfall of revenue. In 1818 it was running a deficit of £13m and nearly 80 per cent of its revenue was used to pay interest on the National Debt. For the three years after the war no action had been taken to correct the deficit and stabilise the finances because MPs had been unwilling to see measures taken which might have damaged their personal financial well-being. They were keen to urge a sharp reduction in expenditure to keep the burden of taxation as low as possible, although there was little the government could do to reduce its level further. There was, as Castlereagh discerned, an 'ignorant impatience of taxation'.

Given the circumstances of acute distress and unpopularity, Liverpool decided in 1819 that he must make the state of the economy his first priority and take action to restore sound finance. Following the recommendations of a Bullion Committee, which included all senior ministers and was chaired by Sir Robert Peel, the government planned a phased return to the Gold Standard. This meant that in future the £ sterling was to be worth a fixed amount of gold. It was hoped that this would help control the inflation brought about by the banks issuing too many notes (any bank could issue paper money at this time) without having the reserves which would enable them to be converted into gold, on demand. The return to gold did have an effect in checking the rise in prices, and is credited by many economic historians with causing an improvement in Britain's foreign exchange position and an inflow of gold to the Bank of England.

In that same year, in a more determined attempt to return to solvency, it was proposed in the Budget to collect £3m more in taxes. This was meant to restore confidence, but beyond this goal, Liverpool recognised the crucial need to give a boost to an ailing economy. He wanted to promote a recovery in manufacturing and trade by lowering tariffs. This was a policy which was to be developed in the early 1820s. Ministers came to see that industry rather than agriculture offered the best prospect of economic growth, and the switch in emphasis enabled the government to widen its support by appealing to representatives of industry and commerce whose interests had been sacrificed in 1815.

f) The Queen Caroline Affair, 1820

In 1820 the Whigs had an opportunity to embarrass the Tory government when a major political scandal broke out. The new king, George IV, had married Princess Caroline of Brunswick in 1795, but their relationship had long since broken down. Caroline lived a flamboyant and scandalous life abroad. However, when George IV came to the throne she was determined to return to England to be crowned as queen. The king was horrified at such a prospect, and he urged Lord Liverpool to assist him in divorcing his wife. The government decided to begin proceedings, and introduced a Bill in parliament (the only way of gaining a divorce at the time) to dissolve the marriage and thereby deprive her of her desired title.

Such was the display of public support for the 'wronged woman' and so unpopular was George that the Bill had to be withdrawn. Caroline received some support from the Whigs. Among the Tories, Canning was so uneasy at the 'persecution' he thought she was enduring that he resigned from the ministry. Lord Liverpool, who had never wished to be drawn into the affair, got a taste of the public mood when the Bill failed. Amidst much rejoicing in the capital, some ministers had the windows of their homes shattered. Caroline soon faded from public attention (and died a year later) but George's reputation never fully recovered. The government had long been very unpopular and, particularly in 1819-20, it was held in low esteem. Shelley expressed popular feeling in his Sonnet, *England,* in which he wrote of 'rulers who neither see, nor feel, nor know'.

The gap between government and governed had been growing wider. Peel observed how out of touch with popular opinion the government had become and noted that though the public possessed more influence than ever before. Of a friend he asked,

1 Do you not think that the tone of England ... is more liberal, to use
  an odious but intelligible phrase, than the policy of the
  government? Do not you think that there is a feeling, becoming
  daily more general and more confirmed ... in favour of some
5 undefined change in the mode of governing the country?

It required a reconstruction of the government to improve its public image.

g) Liberal Toryism

The conventional view of Lord Liverpool's premiership is that in 1821-2 his government moved away from a policy of reaction and that this turning-point introduced a new era of 'Liberal Toryism' which ran from 1822 to 1827. Certainly, in the period before the reconstruction of the ministry the 'tough' attitude towards popular discontent and political radicalism, as well as the introduction of the Corn Laws, suggested a government which was determined to defend the position and privileges of the propertied class. The policies of the 1820s, by contrast, seem to mark a thaw. Yet it would be misleading to assume that the ministry consciously changed its outlook in order to inaugurate a new 'liberal' era.

The change in personnel was a significant one. In January 1822 Peel replaced Sidmouth at the Home Office. Castlereagh, borne down by his labours at the Foreign Office and mercilessly lampooned and abused, broke under the strain and in August 1822 cut his throat with a razor. Canning replaced him in both of his offices. In January 1823 'Prosperity' Robinson replaced Vansittart at the Exchequer and Huskisson became President of the Board of Trade. Some of the old and more reactionary ministers had disappeared, and Canning, Huskisson and Peel, the best-known of the 'new' faces (although they had all served in the Liverpool team in the past), were a welcome addition to the Front Bench in the House of Commons which had lacked prominent members of the Cabinet previously. After the Queen Caroline affair the time was ripe for renewal, and the men appointed appeared to be in touch with the spirit of the time. The changes ushered in a more constructive phase in government policy.

However, it is clear that Liverpool was not consciously embarking upon a change of direction. This view is substantiated by the fact that several of the 'new' policies had been introduced or planned before the change of personnel. For example, Wallace, the energetic Vice-President of the Board of Trade, had started on a programme of complete revision of the commercial system and a move towards free trade, although it is Huskisson who is usually credited with the policies of the mid-1820s. But Liverpool's changes in his team created the impression that a more active policy was now to be pursued. The government looked to be more firmly in control of events.

Because there was an improvement in the prevailing economic climate, the government's attitude seemed to change. At last there was a general state of peace and the tensions associated with turbulence and unrest subsided as the worst years passed into memory. Against this background, and guided by younger and more able men, the administration was more sympathetic to reform. With the decline in public disturbances ministers had more time to devote to reconstruction and reform.

Compared with the 'repression' which went before, the policies pursued between 1822 and 1827 seemed more liberal, although it is easy to exaggerate both the extent and the novelty of the changes. They did not immediately harm the interests of the landed backers of the party nor did they conflict with deeply-held Tory principles or require heavy expenditure. Nonetheless, important work was done by Peel, Huskisson and Robinson at home, and by Canning abroad, as a brief account of their main measures indicates.

h) Huskisson and Robinson

Over the centuries tariffs on many imported goods had been introduced in order to protect industry from overseas competition, and others had been added in order to raise money during the wars against revolutionary France. In 1819 a petition from London merchants pleading for an end to these restrictions was presented to parliament. It was received positively by the Liverpool government which was increasingly willing to move along the road towards free trade.

William Huskisson was a rising figure in the Tory Party. He was an enlightened economist and a believer in freer trade. He accepted the view that the more countries traded with each other the richer they would all become. In his words, 'national prosperity will be most effectually promoted by unrestrained competition not only between ... different classes in the same country, but also by extending that competition as much as possible to all countries'.

In the pursuit of these aims he modified the Navigation Acts which had made it compulsory for all imports to and exports from Britain and the colonies to be carried in English ships or in the ships of the country from which the goods came. From now on ships of all countries could bring in goods. He went further, and lowered some of the duties on goods coming into England, and concluded Reciprocity Treaties with some countries so that there could be a mutually advantageous reduction of tariffs between them.

He was working on a modification of the Corn Laws when he left office, and in this he had the support of Lord Liverpool who had spoken out boldly on agriculture in 1822. Liverpool blamed the post-war distress in the farming community on 'inflation, over-investment and over-production in the war years', and stressed that to bring about recovery it was necessary to see a recovery of the national economy as a whole. He argued that

1 Manufacturing, trade and agriculture are all interdependent, and it is the duty of government and of parliament to hold the balance between all the great interests of the country ... The agricultural is not the only interest in Great Britain. It is not even the most 5 numerous.

The gentry did not like what they heard and were resistant to the prospect of changes in the Corn Laws.

Huskisson was also the minister involved in the repeal of the Combination Laws, which had been introduced by Pitt in 1800 and 1801 and which had forbidden workers to form trades unions or to organise strikes. Repeal was primarily the work of Francis Place, a Radical tailor who won the support of Joseph Hume, an MP. Hume organised the passage of a Bill in parliament in 1824, and neither

Liverpool nor Huskisson fully appreciated the implications of what was being done. After an outbreak of strikes following repeal, the law was modified on the government's instigation in 1825 so that unions were allowed to exist and workers were allowed to strike, but only as long as there was no molestation of workers who did not join.

Overall, Huskisson's economic policy had widened the Tory Party's appeal to include the moderate centre ground. His work between 1822 and 1827 marks him out as a Tory reformer, for he had taken the first significant steps along the road to free trade. Somewhat tragically, he did not live to see many further steps taken, for in 1830 he unwisely stepped in front of a locomotive at the opening ceremony of the Manchester-Liverpool Railway, with fatal results.

Huskisson's work was complemented by that of Robinson at the Exchequer. For a while he presided over a more successful economy, although to a considerable extent this reflected the improvement in trading conditions which had come about since 1819 rather than any action he had taken. At first he was able to balance the budget while reducing taxation. For example, in 1823 there were a number of tax reductions, especially on items likely to be bought by the rich, for Robinson believed that their prosperity would ultimately benefit the whole community. His argument was that if the well-to-do were encouraged to create more wealth, they would then be in a position to take on more workingmen as employees. The concessions were extended to more basic commodities such as coal and wool in the following year, and the Chancellor of the Exchequer was awarded his nickname 'Prosperity Robinson' as a result. When conditions took a turn for the worse in 1825, and a slump in exports caused a deterioration of the national finances, some of the gloss of his reputation wore off.

i) Peel at the Home Office

Sir Robert Peel tackled the savage penal system. Some of the punishments inflicted by the law courts had been most severe and in 1819 alone nearly 10,000 criminals had been transported to Botany Bay in Australia. More than 200 crimes, including pick-pocketing, were punishable by death, but increasingly the penalties did not have the deterrent effect intended as juries had become reluctant to convict because of the harshness of the law. Often they refused to condemn a person to death for stealing property of little value. Sir Samuel Romilly and Sir James Mackintosh had long campaigned for reform, and Peel took up their ideas so that the death penalty was removed from more than 180 offences and the whole penal system was made more humane. No longer were suicide victims to be buried at the crossroads with a stake through their hearts! Mackintosh later commented on the changed situation: 'I could almost think I had lived in two different countries'.

Peel was similarly active in other areas, and in this period the Gaols

Act (1823) improved conditions in the insanitary and overcrowded prisons of the larger towns and cities. Regular inspection was to take place and the prisons' administration was to be drastically revised. However, it was the setting up of the Metropolitan Police Force for which Peel is best remembered as Home Secretary. For several years he had been convinced that it was necessary to have a regular police force in London, despite the fears of those who were anxious about a threat to the traditional liberties of Englishmen. He realised that the existing arrangements were grossly inadequate. But it was not until 1829 that he was able to gain enough support for his constructive reform.

It had been Peel's ambition to bequeath 'some record of the trust I have held which may outlive the fleeting discharge of the mere duties of ordinary routine, and that may perhaps confer some distinction on my name, by connecting it with permanent improvements in the judicial institutions of the country'. He had proceeded cautiously, for he feared that too hasty an approach might have created a 'strong prejudice ... against measures that were intended for the public good; and thus the great object of justice and humanity might be defeated'. His innovations, when they came, were not the product of his own thinking, for he rarely had novel ideas himself. However, he did excel in translating the ideas of others into practical effect. He listened well and was open to persuasion.

j) Canning at the Foreign Office, 1822-7

George Canning was the Tory held in the highest popular esteem, and during his period as Foreign Secretary British policy took on a more liberal tinge. He was disliked by the reactionary clique of statesmen who governed in Europe, and gained a reputation as the enemy of kings and the friend of peoples. This was partly because of his work in supporting the cause of liberty and constitutionalism in Greece, Portugal and Spain, but particularly because of his backing for the freedom and independence of the South American republics which were in the process of breaking away from the Spanish empire. Gladstone was later to describe him as the first English friend of peoples struggling for their freedom. The historian H.A.L. Fisher was similarly impressed by his achievements, and concluded that 'he was in foreign policy an exponent of the new type of popular and liberal diplomacy'.

Canning's emphasis on the 'Englishness' of his approach and his willingness to ignore the niceties of diplomacy went down well with many people. His attitude and manner, and his attempt to make foreign policy popular and intelligible, made him seem more progressive than he was. A glance at his record in home affairs casts some doubt on the reality of his liberalism. True, he did support Catholic Emancipation, but he had also defended the magistrates at Peterloo in remarks that could have come from the mouth of Lord Sidmouth, and he had supported the Six Acts. He also opposed any reform of the criminal law and of the electoral system,

Yet for all of the limitations of his views on domestic policy, his presence in the government was reassuring to those who wanted to see reform. He was highly intelligent and had shrewdly cultivated public opinion. The Whig Lord Brougham (pronounced 'Broom') noted one useful gift that he possessed. 'He was an actor, a first-rate one no doubt, but still an actor'. He had the 'gift of the gab', and could sell his policies. He contrived to take credit for any of the government's reforms that were popular, whilst detaching himself from the odium of any that were less pleasing.

k) The End of the Liverpool Ministry

In February 1827 Liverpool resigned following a stroke. He died a year later. His reputation had often been attacked, and literary radicals such as Byron and Shelley condemned his government in the years immediately after 1815 as reactionary and repressive. Such terms are still used by some historians today - if only to provide a contrast with the approach to government in the 1820s.

Those on the political Left are apt to stress the sinister use of police spies and *agents provocateurs,* the lack of any real attempt to relieve distress, and the government's reactions to the tragedy of Peterloo. Those on the Right are more prone to concentrate on the difficulties in which the government found itself and to show that in their attitudes they were representative of the thinking men of their time. They stress that ministers were dealing with problems of immense complexity, including those of a nascent industrial society at the end of a long war.

Brock, in *Lord Liverpool and Liberal Toryism,* which although published in 1941 is still highly regarded, noted that the Prime Minister was,

> 1 Representative of his age in a way that few statesmen have been, for
>   he reflected both its prejudices and its enlightenment in exact
>   proportions ... He seems, at one moment, to be looking back to the
>   eighteenth century, at another to have set his face towards the
> 5 prosperous commercial world of the nineteenth century.

Throughout his premiership he pursued a conservative policy which was to provide the basis for the new Conservative Party of Sir Robert Peel - a moderate coalition of those who favoured cautious reform combined with a strong defence of law and order. To judge him only by his response to radical discontent is to ignore his more constructive approach, especially after 1819, in economic policy and the other changes in domestic policy over which he presided in the 1820s. The true measure of his achievement as a party leader was to become more apparent after his passing from the scene, when his conciliatory gifts were much missed and no one else could maintain harmony between the various personalities and factions within the Tory Party.

l) The Break-up of Liberal Toryism

On Liverpool's death George IV invited Canning to become Prime Minister. Several High Tories (and Peel, who disagreed with Canning over Catholic Emancipation) immediately resigned from the government so that the new Prime Minister had to include some Whigs in his ministry in order to fill all the vacancies. In 1827 he was widely admired, respected by many as a genuine liberal, and his government was perhaps the most enlightened in tone for 20 years. However, Canning was not in office long enough to tackle the major issue of the time - the Catholic problem - for by August of the same year he was dead.

Robinson, now known as Lord Goderich, briefly succeeded Canning, and this intelligent and popular man headed a government similar in composition to that of its predecessor. As a Prime Minister Goderich was weak and easily bullied by his colleagues, whom he could not control. He even broke down in the act of offering to resign. George proffered his pocket handkerchief and accepted the resignation.

By comparison, his successor, the Duke of Wellington, was a 'strong' man. His administration included Peel back at the Home Office and for a while the Canningites remained. Eventually, after a wrangle concerning redistribution of parliamentary seats, the more reforming elements, including Huskisson, resigned in 1828. Technically their resignation marks the end of the era of Liberal Toryism for some of the more progressive Tories such as Lord Palmerston, who had held minor office since 1809, went over to the Whig side to lay the foundations of the nineteenth-century Liberal Party.

m) Wellington as Prime Minister

After the exit of the 'progressives', much depended on Wellington and Peel. The duke was a stubborn man of narrow vision and little intellectual consistency. His speeches were those of a High Tory who believed that the British constitution was perfect. Yet he had a strong sense of duty and his devotion to the nation's welfare was unquestionable. He was ultimately willing to adapt his policy to bring it in line with the needs of the day, for he usually knew when the time had come to give way.

His ministry accomplished some useful changes, notably the establishment of the Metropolitan Police. However, it soon fell to Wellington's government to deal with the Catholic question and this issue wrecked any remaining unity within the Tory Party. The prelude to Emancipation was the passage of a bill which repealed the Test and

Corporations Act with respect to Protestant Dissenters (Non-conformists) who in reality had been able to assume public office and take a parliamentary seat for many years as this particular law had been a dead letter for a long time. However, this tidying up measure was watched with interest by Roman Catholics for their disabilities were never likely to be removed as long as Dissenters were, in theory at least, bound by them.

The government was in an acute dilemma over the Catholic question. Daniel O'Connell had been elected as MP for County Clare in Ireland but because he was a Roman Catholic he was unable to take his seat at Westminster. There was much excitement and the prospect of violent disorder throughout Ireland if O'Connell were to be permanently denied the right to serve as an MP. The situation would be even worse if at the next election more Catholics were returned and similarly debarred. Wellington had consistently endorsed a strongly Protestant position and had been opposed to any measure of Catholic Emancipation, but with aristocratic pessimism he was now prepared to give way in the current circumstances. Peel was in a more difficult position. He had been a passionate and unbending opponent of Emancipation, to which he had ably led much of the opposition. He would have preferred to leave the government so that Emancipation could be introduced by those who either really believed in it, or at least were less hostile to it than he was. However, he had a strong sense of loyalty to the Prime Minister and was persuaded by him to remain in office.

There was no half-way house on this question. The government must either resist Irish pressure, with all the attendant dangers of so doing, or accept the reality of the situation and bring in repeal. In 1829 Peel introduced the measure in the House of Commons, and Wellington used his influence in the Lords to persuade colleagues to relent in their opposition. In both chambers there was a massive revolt against the leadership, with 198 MPs and 116 Peers voting against the party line. Nonetheless, as a result of their effort, Catholic Emancipation was passed. In the process Peel's reputation suffered a grievous blow for, along with Wellington, he was accused of betraying the Tory Party. However, he felt that he was acting appropriately,

1 The events of the Clare election [when O'Connell was elected], with the conviction that the same scenes would be enacted in nearly every county in Ireland if matters were to remain just as they have been for the last five or six years, convinced me that it was not 5 safe for the Protestant interest in Ireland that they should remain so.

His critics were unimpressed by his stance and alleged that he had changed his name from 'R. Peel to Repeal'. As far as they were concerned he had clung on to office despite abandoning the firm principles he had consistently espoused. They believed that, in clinging to office, he was sacrificing Tory principles to personal ambition. On this occasion he was able to survive the growing suspicion of him, but he was to be unable to repeat this success when another issue came up in his career which posed the same question - whether it is appropriate in politics to change one's mind on an important issue and yet to remain in office (see pages 62-8).

A few months later the ministry fell when all of its enemies lined up against it. The Tories were in disarray and in no position to survive a critical vote in the House, for they were hopelessly divided. There were by this time three broad groups within the party:

1   the remaining ex-Canningites, a more progressive group on the left, who did not, however, always act in unison;
2   the centre, which followed Peel and Wellington, and accepted the inevitability of moderate and reasonable change;
3   the Ultras who opposed change of any kind.

So large was the group of Ultras that according to Frank O'Gorman in *The Emergence of the British Two-Party System* it constituted 'a party within a party'. It had the sympathy of the king and the Tory press, and was attempting to 'convert the all-inclusive Toryism of Liverpool, Peel and Wellington into a narrow, coherent, well-organised and popularly-supported anti-reform Tory party'.

However, those on the Tory side who had up until then opposed parliamentary reform were losing their cohesion. Whilst the bulk of the party rejected any change in the electoral system, some believed that a more representative House of Commons would have never allowed the passage of Catholic Emancipation and were therefore prepared to support a moderate measure of reform.

n) Parliamentary Reform and the 1832 Act

In 1830 the Whigs took office. When a Reform Bill was introduced, the Tories opposed the measure. This was because, whereas the Whigs felt that in the excited circumstances of the time some repair-work to the constitution was necessary, the Tories mostly saw such a change as undesirable. Ultras opposed it outright, for they disapproved of almost all reform on principle and believed that further concessions must inevitably be for the worse. Less extreme Tories saw dangers in parliamentary reform because they felt that it would disturb the balance of the constitution. Peel shared this view. His anxiety was that any measure of reform would ultimately lead to Britain becoming a democratic state based on universal franchise, as a door would be opened which, once ajar, would be impossible to close again.

The Whig proposals were not dramatically far-reaching, but on their publication one Tory speaker introduced a theme which was to be endlessly repeated. He claimed that the bill was 'a revolution that will overturn all the natural influence of rank and property'. Other points were added subsequently. The proposed reform was seen as an exercise in 'robbery and pillage' in that it threatened private property by eliminating those boroughs which were controlled by landed patrons. It was argued that it would transfer power from the gentry to the industrial classes, for 'the field of coal would beat the field of barley', and that it would introduce a system in which there were just as many anomalies as before. Above all, however, there was the fear that this reform would be followed by more reform, and that the innovations would not just affect the electoral system, but that they would also ultimately change other institutions as well. Thus the monarchy, the Lords, the Church, and private property were claimed to be under threat as well. As one critic put it, 'all will be levelled to the plane of the petty shopkeeper and small farmer'.

Whatever the merits of the Tory case, it did not meet the needs of the immediate situation. It was true that this measure could never be a final measure, but in 1832 some reform was a practical necessity - just as Catholic Emancipation had been in 1829. The new voters endorsed the Whig bill when it became law in 1832, for in December of that year they gave the party a large majority, and inflicted on the Tories their worst defeat in the nineteenth century.

The years between 1815 and 1832 were significant ones in the history of the Tory Party. After Liverpool's retirement the party seriously split as it encountered a number of contentious issues. The dilemma of many conservatives came to the surface in their reaction to them. Should they bow to the inevitable when changes were needed, or should they fight in the last ditch to defend their principles and position? Might reform lead to revolution, or was it the case that acceptance of reform when the time was prudent would stave off catastrophe?

There were many Tories, such as Lord Eldon, who favoured fighting a rearguard action and who could not stand the approach of those who bent with the wind and made concessions. However, it was the Liverpools, the Huskissons and the Peels, or those like them in attitude, who dominated the party's direction and had responsibility for its strategy. They ensured that Conservatives knew when it was time to adapt to the needs and realities of the time.

3 Organisational Matters

Until 1832 Tory party organisation was of a very basic kind, 'a loose and sporadic co-operation between like-minded people to achieve some common purpose'. Few people were involved, policies and tactics were the preserve of the great men in the party, and the leaders rarely met with their supporters. Occasionally, there were meetings at which the leaders might explain their thinking or strategy, or more likely plead for better attendance. There they could seek to enthuse their supporters to win them round, although some leaders saw no necessity to do so.

Apart from regular parliamentary life at Westminster, there were many informal gatherings in clubs and private houses where political discussion could and did take place. Insights and gossip would be exchanged over the dining tables of fashionable houses, where grandees who were not in parliament and Tory or Whig hostesses could make their views known.

a) Life at Westminster

In the House of Commons custom dictated that ministers occupied the front benches to the right of the Speaker, with leading members of the other side on the front benches facing them; supporters ranged themselves on the backbenches behind. Party leaders were not elected, and Lord Liverpool was chosen as leader only after he had been appointed as Prime Minister. As the Prime Minister could only sit in one House he normally appointed a leader for the other one, either by his own decision or after discussion with several of the party notables. In this way Liverpool made Castlereagh his leader of the House of Commons after due consultation.

The leader appointed the Whips, whose main responsibility was keeping MPs in line. The idea of whipping, in parliamentary terms, derived from the hunting-field where a person is designated to whip in the hounds which 'straggle' from the pack. It was Burke who was credited with first applying the label to the party officials responsible for maintaining order in the party but their role at his time was still in its infancy.

On the government side the Whips were salaried. It was the duty of the Chief Whip and his three or four assistants to ensure sufficient co-operation and loyalty to the government of the day to enable it to survive divisions in the House of Commons. Often clubable country gentlemen, they were discreet and well-fitted to persuade people of their own background to follow where the leadership wished to go. Their role involved keeping in touch with the backbenchers, bringing dissidents into line and mustering a good turn-out for parliamentary divisions. They sent letters to their known parliamentary supporters outlining future business in the Commons and advising them of the preferred way of casting their vote. The Chief Whip sometimes combined his role with that of Patronage Secretary to the Treasury. As such he could dispense offices and pensions as rewards for loyal service, so that there was always the prospect of advancement for loyal supporters.

Despite the best efforts of the whips, the House of Commons was difficult to control and MPs were only reluctantly brought into line. The government could count on only just over 100 or so totally dependable members (about 80 of whom held posts in the administration), and had to seek support from many who were either loose supporters of the party in power or who were uncommitted. The voting of MPs was difficult to predict and MPs could not be relied upon to be present when needed. Often the country gentry would support the Liverpool government, although this support could not be counted on as the 1820s progressed. That they did generally do so until then was largely because of a fear of letting in the Whig alternative. In *The Whigs in Opposition*, Mitchell produced some surprising figures which showed that Liverpool could get the support he needed, for many MPs were consistent in their voting habits, despite their unreliability.

Parliament	Govt	Govt fringe	Waverers	Opp fringe	Opposition
1812-18	253	78	102	83	149
1818-20	261	80	48	16	171
1820-26	250	99	114	66	154

The number of independent MPs seems to have been on the increase in the late 1820s, and the search for a majority then had to be conducted more carefully. Throughout the period various temporary alliances of individuals and groups were formed around particular issues, such as over Catholic Emancipation and parliamentary reform, although, in as much as the majority of MPs felt beholden to anyone, it was more likely to be to the patron who controlled their seat and whose influence had helped to get them elected than to their party.

b) Political Associations and Party Development

Political parties did not extend to the country at large; such organisation was unnecessary as so few people had the vote. However, there were a vast number of voluntary associations for political purposes which sought to persuade parliament to effect particular reforms, but there was little liaison between societies in the country and the parties at Westminster. The societies existed for specific and limited objects rather than for the promotion of a political programme covering all aspects of national life. There had been bodies campaigning for parliamentary reform, such as the Yorkshire Association and the Society for Constitutional Information, but these had usually been short-lived. Generally after 1815 the societies which existed were seeking a major piece of legislation. When they had achieved it they tended to disband. They also tended, by their very nature, to be on the radical side, for they were seeking change and reform.

Government and opposition MPs had made much of their dead heroes who became highly revered figures. Foxite and Pittite Clubs had been established to perpetuate their memory. Pitt Clubs, which were the more widespread, were determined to preserve the name of Pitt, and idealised his performance and achievement. After Waterloo they were strident in their demands for tough government action and strong sentences from the magistrates. The cult remained for several years, and dinners, anniversaries and the production of numerous biographies and portraits kept the memory alive.

c) Parties in the Constituencies

The early years of organised party activity were overwhelmingly concentrated on Westminster. Locally, around the country, the picture is a confusing one. In some areas, such as Hampshire, there had been candidates using the party names of Whig and Tory as far back as 1806-7. O'Gorman has shown that in about half of the English counties, party labels were being employed in the 1820s. Activity was often not continuous, and it was purely local in inspiration. It tended to increase in times of political excitement, as in the years 1829-32. Again, within the boroughs, the picture is not clear-cut. In some boroughs the labels were occasionally used, even if the causes espoused bore little relation to what was being said and done nationally. In some seats there was regular party rivalry, as at Lichfield where two local families dominated affairs, one on each side of the political divide. In a very few larger boroughs there was more marked activity in which either side identified more closely with the views expressed by representatives at Westminster.

However, such conflict was normally parochial and it was not until the early 1830s that the national parties made an effort to organise their supporters and voters in parts of the country via their headquarters in London. As the Tories organised their resistance to parliamentary reform, they developed central institutions to run the party, notably the Carlton Club in 1832, of which we will hear more later.

Nevertheless, O'Gorman concluded his survey of the scene before the Reform Act by saying that:

1 Few constituencies were without their clubs and societies, their rituals and their calendars of birth-dates, anniversaries and celebrations. These clubs were the local agencies of party organisation before central party institutions reached out to touch
5 the constituencies ... Some, a minority, used the words 'Whig' and 'Tory'. Others used the ... terminology of colours, the Yellows v the Blues of Ipswich, for example. In others, the enigmatic 'Constitutional Club' might find itself in conflict with the 'Independent Club'.

Repression	**Liberal Toryism**	**Disintegration and Defeat**

Lord Liverpool PM
1815-22

Lord Liverpool PM
1822-7

1827-32

Problems - effects of French
Revolution
- effects of Industrial
Revolution
- high unemployment
- growing population

Reconstruction of
Cabinet 1822-7

Death of Liverpool 1827

'Liberal'
men in key
offices

⎛Huskisson
⎜Robinson
⎝Peel
   Canning

Canning and
Goderich PMs
1827-8

Aggravated by   - Corn Laws 1815
Government   - indirect taxes
Action/Inaction - lack of parlia-
mentary reform

Wellington PM
1828-30
- Catholic
Emancipation 1829

Matched by
'Liberal' - Canning
Foreign Policy

Discontent - Spa Fields 1816
- Peterloo 1819
- Cato St. Conspiracy 1820

1830 Election Defeat

Opposition 1830-2 -
Parliamentary Reform

Repressive
Measures

- suspension of *Habeas
Corpus* 1817
- Six Acts 1819

1832 Electoral Catastrophe

Summary - The Tories, 1815-32

Making notes on *'The Tories, 1815-32'*

The most important political figure during this period was Lord Liverpool. Construct your notes around his personality and his policies. Distinguish between the period when his policies are often described as 'repressive' (1815-22) and the years in which his approach is described as more 'liberal' (1822-7). The following headings will help you to organise your thinking;

1815-22   Leading members of the Cabinet and their outlook
The social and economic problems of the time
The extent and gravity of discontent

How the government handled disorder

The distinction between political and economic Toryism

The arguments For and Against the 'repressive' interpretation

1822-7   The attitude and work of the main 'liberal Tories' (you should have a set of notes on Huskisson, Robinson, Peel and Canning)

Lord Liverpool - assessment of his contribution to party and country

For the period after Liverpool's resignation it is probably most helpful to adopt a straightforward chronological approach.

1827-8   Ministries and their composition; listed summary

1828-30   Wellington - his outlook

Main reforms - a brief summary

Catholic Emancipation, 1829. In making your notes, ensure that you include a section on the approach of Peel and Wellington. Ask yourself whether Peel was right to change his mind on this issue

1830-2   Parliamentary Reform; the differing attitudes of Tories

---

Answering essay question on 'The Tories, 1815-32'

Questions on the years up to 1822 are normally based on the reaction of Liverpool's government to distress and discontent. For example:

1   To what extent did the policies of Liverpool's government provoke the unrest in the years after 1815 and how effectively did it handle it?

To answer this question successfully you need to provide a succinct summary of the causes of distress and of the disorders which broke out. But do not allow yourself to be immersed in the details of the Corn Laws or of Peterloo and other demonstrations. Concentrate on what they indicate about the state of the country, whether it was in a state of revolutionary unease, and whether the government's policies actually worsened the situation and 'provoked the unrest'.

The question asks 'To what extent?'. Examiners do not use such terms merely to vary one question from another; the phrase is a vital part of the whole, and tells you how you need to use your information. In this case, your evidence in the early paragraphs will explain that there were ample reasons for discontent. Later paragraphs will show how, via legislation and 'repressive' means of control, the government aggravated, even if did not cause, the situation. Depending on how much the weight of your evidence has demonstrated the government's responsibility, in your conclusion you will be able to determine the 'extent' of its culpability.

A more challenging question would be:

> 2   On what grounds can the repressive policies of the Liverpool government between 1815-22 be defended?

One of the key words in this question is 'repressive', which seems to convict the government before its policies have been explained and analysed. In your introductory paragraph you should either challenge or qualify the word, although you may conclude that it is a convenient label to use.

A visual plan can be a useful means of preparing an essay, and it has the advantage that points can be added as new thoughts arise. Such a plan helps to allow you to develop a logical argument. It is the analysis and evaluation rather than an excess of detail which will help you to score well, so you need to balance fact and comment, using the former to substantiate the latter. Overloading fact tends to bury the argument, and the examiner is interested in your ability to adapt your information to the demands of the question set. Discipline yourself to be selective in your use of factual material.

See whether the form of plan on page 47 helps you to arrange your material for the essay above (such a diagrammatic approach can also be an aid to revision).

Essays are also set on the so-called 'liberal' Tories. For example you might be invited to assess:

> 3   How liberal were the 'liberal' Tories of 1822 to 1827/8/30?

Pay special attention to the end-date given in such questions. '1827' stops with Liverpool and possibly Canning, while '1830' includes Wellington whose outlook may seem markedly illiberal. Yet, were not useful reforms accomplished between 1828-30? Come to a decision about when you think liberal Toryism, if it really ever existed, came to an end.

You might be asked an overall question on Liverpool, such as:

> 4   Discuss the view that 'Lord Liverpool was an outstanding Prime Minister given the problems of his time'.

Your response needs to be in two parts; an assessment of the problems he faced (in both periods) as well as a discussion of his qualities and contribution. Ask yourself whether there was a genuine change in the character and performance of the government around 1820, and if so why it came about. How, if at all, might he have handled the conduct of government more effectively?

On what grounds can the policies of Lord Liverpool's Government of 1815–22 be defended?

Introduction

Government widely seen by historians/contemporaries (Shelley) as repressive. Fair?

Why need defending e.g. handling of difficult post-war situation

Measures employed, some of which aggravated position. Corn Laws, Indirect Taxes, lack of Parliamentary Reform

Attitude to situation equated discontent with conspiracy and rebellion – some Ministers responded with 'repressive' measures *Habeas Corpus*, 6 Acts, *Agents Provocateurs*

Yet attitude surprising? Near to French Revolution, still in memory – some Ministers witnessed it. Fear of 'deluded people' roused by Radical orators

Also, Nature of Problems; very difficult – nascent industrial society, unemployment

Lack of understanding: no knowledge of what could be done. Who did know? Whigs? Contemporary *laissez-faire* philosophy

Government may have been out of touch (Peel's comment) and lacking comprehension but not 'sinister or repressive' as portrayed

Furthermore, if political Toryism uninspiring, did develop economic thinking after 1819 – tentative move to Free Trade

Conclusion Policies can be defended, even if without enthusiasm. Faced by daunting problems, uninspired. As economic circumstances improved, and Lord Liverpool appointed 'new', more 'liberal' ministers after 1821, Government moved into more constructive phase

Source-based questions on 'The Tories, 1815-32'

1 The Plea of the Birmingham Artisans
Carefully read the extract on pages 27-8. Answer the following questions:
a) What were the problems faced by the distressed artisans of Birmingham? (5 marks)
b) What similarities were there between the grievances of the Birmingham artisans and those of people elsewhere in the country? (pages 24-7 and the extract on pages 27-8) (5 marks)
c) Compare the views of the Birmingham artisans on the causes of their distress and the ways in which it ought to be tackled with those of Liverpool and Sidmouth. (5 marks)
d) What can we learn about the attitude of the Birmingham artisans to those in authority over them from the language and tone of the extract? (5 marks)

2 James Ings, Cato Street Conspirator
Carefully read the extract on page 28. Answer the following questions.
a) Why, in your opinion, was Ings particularly keen to have the heads of Castlereagh and Sidmouth? (4 marks)
b) To what extent did his remarks confirm the government's view of the cause of the discontent in the country at large? (4 marks)
c) Compare Ings' approach with that of the Birmingham artisans as described in the extract on pages 27-8. (6 marks)
d) How typical was Ings' approach of that of those who opposed the government? (6 marks)

3 Lord Liverpool and Free Trade
Carefully read the information on pages 24 and 29-30 and the extract on page 33. Answer the following questions.
a) What was Liverpool's attitude towards the agricultural interest in 1815? (4 marks)
b) How had his attitude changed by the early 1820s? (4 marks)
c) What evidence do the extracts provide to suggest that Lord Liverpool was sympathetic to free trade? (5 marks)
d) In what ways does Lord Liverpool's thinking on free trade indicate that he was representative of the 'prejudice and the enlightenment' of his age? (3 marks)
e) Using evidence from the extracts and from the text of the chapter, compare the attitudes of Huskisson and Liverpool to free trade in agriculture. (4 marks)

CHAPTER 4

Conservatism, 1832-46: The Age of Peel

1 Introduction

After the passing of the 1832 Reform Act it was Peel's task to create a new political grouping. This soon became known as the Conservative Party. The term had been used sporadically over several years, and was of continental origin. Its use was usually in the French form, as when Wellington spoke in 1827 of the *parti conservateur* in the country. Three years later an anonymous writer in the *Quarterly Review* noted that, 'We now are, as we always have been, decidedly and conscientiously attached to what is called the Tory, and which might with more propriety be called, the Conservative Party'.

By December 1831 the *Standard* (a daily newspaper) was using 'Conservative' as if it was widely understood, and certainly between 1830 and 1832 it was more frequently used as the label to denote those who stood for the conservation of ancient British institutions. However, it was only after the Reform Act that the word 'Conservative' entered into regular use.

Its adoption by politicians and writers was a deliberate attempt to purge the party of its old associations and the change implied a modest alteration of direction. The word 'Tory' had some odious connections. It was a reminder of the dark days after 1815, of the Peterloo massacre, and of governments which had seemed to be dedicated to the defence of privilege and property. Now was the time to broaden the party's appeal and to reach out to a wider section of the community. 'Conservative' had a milder nuance, suggesting the preservation of the best of the past, whilst in no way implying absolute hostility to reform.

To be seen as an anti-reformer after 1832 was unlikely to do much for one's electoral prospects. True, some older members did still like to be thought of as good, old-fashioned Tories, and it was the king's brother, the Duke of Cumberland, who remarked in 1830 that, 'Any change, at any time, is highly to be deprecated'. Peel viewed things differently. For him, Conservatism should 'be compatible with cautious and well-digested reforms in every institution which really requires reform, and with redress of proven grievances'.

As such, the new name stressed the need for political and social stability to protect society from 'that bloody anarchy striding towards us'. It would appeal to those 'responsible' elements who wished to defend the constitution from subversion and resist dangerous and radical encroachments. Yet it would also enable the party to pursue the path of cautious reform.

2 Policies and Personalities

The Tory Party went out of office in 1830 and two years later it suffered the most shattering defeat in its history - it was reduced to a rump of 185 MPs. Even in the counties, traditionally a stronghold of Conservatism, years of agricultural depression had taken their toll, and the party won only 42 of the 144 seats. Most of its support came from the smaller boroughs of less than 1,000 voters. The Tories won in only 8 of the larger urban constituencies. The expanded electorate had rewarded the Whigs for their willingness to concede parliamentary reform and had punished the Tories for their flat refusal to entertain it. The Tories were humiliated and had to find a way of attracting the voters who had been enfranchised by the 1832 Act. In England and Wales it was only the middle classes who had been given the vote and the party had to broaden its appeal to them. It was to do so on the basis of Conservatism, rather than on the basis of Toryism which was identified in the public mind with absolute hostility to reform.

When the first reformed parliament met in 1832 there was no recognised Conservative leader. As an ex-prime minister, Wellington was still a key figure, politically active in the House of Lords. However, he had made it clear that he was not interested in resuming the premiership. Peel was undoubtedly the leading Conservative in the House of Commons but some discontented Ultras had reservations about formally accepting him as their leader. It was not until the political crisis of 1834, when the king dismissed Lord Melbourne as his First Minister, that Peel's position was settled beyond any doubt. On Wellington's advice, William IV sent for Peel and asked him to form a government. He was to guide the party for more than a decade, with responsibility for both its policy and its parliamentary tactics. He was indisputably the man in charge and only a major revolt would have pitched him out. He exercised great influence on his parliamentary party, determined the general direction in which it moved and re-united supporters in the House of Commons. He provided the drive and was aware that the future of the party was, in Briggs's phrase, 'bound up in him'.

a) Peel's Personality

'A constitutional statesman is, in general, a man of common opinions and uncommon abilities'. So wrote the nineteenth-century political commentator Walter Bagehot with reference to Sir Robert Peel. The description is a very appropriate one, for if his views were unremarkable, often the product of other men's ideas, his personal qualities were in many ways outstanding. Bagehot was not an uncritical admirer of Peel, finding many aspects of his outlook distasteful, but the remark emphasises the pre-eminence of the man. Peel was undoubtedly the dominant Conservative, indeed the dominant politician, of his age. His career symbolised the acceptance of the new men made possible by the growth of manufacturing: '[it] meant the replacement of a class born to rule by men whose own effort constituted their title to place'. For the Peels were middle class. By instinct and background, Peel was a product of the Industrial Revolution. His father, a firm, domineering Conservative, had made a fortune as a mill owner, and the advantages of wealth meant that the son could benefit from the best education that money could buy.

If Peel began with advantages, he climbed to the top because of his ability. Like his father he was very industrious. He was a model son who wished to live up to his family's high expectations of him. He was honest and determined, and used his obvious talents to the full. He was educated at Harrow, where he was a friend of Byron, and then at Oxford University, where the two men were again contemporaries. As students they were of highly contrasting style. One, later the poet and romantic, had flair, imagination and spontaneous impulses. The other, the future prime minister, was shy, withdrawn and intelligent in a methodical sort of way; he worked with continuous application. As Byron later put it, 'I was always in scrapes, Peel never'. Peel was the first student to gain a double first in Maths and Classics, an achievement of outstanding merit. As much of the work was examined orally, before an audience as well as the examiners, it was a daunting experience for all concerned. It required a fine memory, a sharp mind and great clarity of expression. These were just the attributes which Peel possessed.

In his adult life those qualities of his youth remained with Peel. His industry, his mastery of a mass of even complex material, his great understanding and common sense, were apparent to all who knew him, as was his unquestionable integrity. Lord Sidmouth, once a colleague and latterly an opponent, paid tribute to that 'great, powerful, laborious intellect, that unflinching diligence'. Disraeli, who found some aspects of his manner distasteful, noted that 'he was gifted with the faculty of method in the highest degree; and with great powers of application which were sustained by a prodigious memory'. But Peel's was not a fertile or constructive mind; rather, it was essentially practical, concerned with the pressing circumstances and preoccupied with the details of the case. Disraeli went on to observe that,

1 Thus gifted and thus accomplished, Sir Robert Peel had a great deficiency; he was without imagination ... No-one was more sagacious when dealing with the circumstances before him; no-one penetrated the present with more acuteness and accuracy. His
5 judgement was faultless, provided he had not to deal with the future.

It was a mind of narrow range, interested in the techniques of application rather than the discovery of principle. As one writer put it, 'the passion for perfection of detail tended to make him more interested in the way in which a thing was done than in the larger aspects of the thing he was doing'.

Most who knew him found him aloof and cold, which led the Irish MP Daniel O'Connell to compare his smile to the gleam on the silver plate of a coffin lid. Lord Ashley, who never got on with him, found him 'like an iceberg, with a slight thaw on the surface'. His manner was awkward, for he was by nature reticent, and was only at ease in the House of Commons or in the companionship of his family. Many found him humourless, but he could laugh heartily, for example, as he recounted a bawdy story with a group of young and close associates. They found him warm and considerate, and after his death the Duke of Newcastle claimed that he 'could never take a step in public life without reflecting how he [Peel] would have thought of it'. Gladstone was even more complimentary, 'Taken all round, he was the greatest man I have ever known'.

Significantly, after his death he commanded even more respect than when he was alive. By then the less comfortable features of his personality could be more easily overlooked. He was not an easy man for he had a fiery temper, often described as 'peppery'. He was proud and sensitive, and easily wounded by attacks on him. He was often egotistical, given to employing the first person as he laid down what he thought was the appropriate line to take. This made him often overbearing, and he could be a prig. He was convinced of his own rightness, and believed that if something had to be done, then probably he was the best man to do it. He was regarded, even by party supporters, with a degree of suspicion. He never sought to win them round, a trait which was to leave him dangerously exposed in the more difficult moments of his career. More conciliation and charm in such times would have done him a power of good; often, his manner seemed to increase the antagonism of those whom he led.

In the House of Commons he was relaxed, and as a speaker he had considerable gifts. He never lost traces of his Lancashire accent, but he had worked to overcome his lack of confidence on social occasions and to achieve self-control. So convincing was his performance that Disraeli could say that Peel's voice was one of the two most perfect things he had ever known - which makes one wonder what the other was! He was a skilful debater, and if he rarely reached the heights of impassioned oratory, he even more rarely produced an unworthy performance. He was masterly in expounding a case, and his speeches could sway the outcome of a debate, though he persuaded men less by the quality of his argument than by the brilliance of the manner in which it was stated. Disraeli had doubts about his performance as party leader but two years after his death could pronounce him to have been 'the greatest Member of Parliament that ever lived'.

b) The Road to Recovery

Peel accepted that the 1832 Reform Act was irreversible, and that his party must learn to live with it. He recognised that old-fashioned attitudes were doomed to failure and that the Tories needed to broaden their appeal to attract moderate opinion, especially that of the industrial middle classes. He saw that there was nothing to be gained from clinging to the attitudes of the Wellingtonian era. Some of his landowning supporters would have liked to put the clock back to the situation before the extension of the franchise, and stayed loyal to the old policy of 'Protectionism, Protestantism and No Popery'. This would have done nothing to rally middle-of-the-road voters, and would have left the Tories as a narrow-based, largely aristocratic rump, destined for eventual oblivion.

Peel's first speech to the reformed parliament committed him to an acceptance of the Reform Act and to the need for gradual reform. It was a fine performance which showed his pre-eminence on the Opposition side of the House. He seemed to be a figure around whom some Tories and many more moderate Conservatives might rally. He was less pessimistic about future prospects than the Duke of Wellington, and his performance and outlook helped to build up party morale. It was now his task to create a new party from the wreckage of 1832. This presented him with a serious problem of leadership, for some of the younger and more progressive members of the Tory Party had gone over to the Whig side in 1830, whilst on the traditional wing he was viewed with distrust and hostility because of his change of mind over Catholic Emancipation.

Out of the disarray on his backbenches he needed to rebuild party strength by reconstructing the old Tory Party into a new and more appealing creation. The theme was to be moderate reform within the spirit of the constitution. This was a position which would appeal to that section of the community, as yet not Conservative, which was anxious about the threat of disorder and dangerous radical innovation, but which was well-disposed to peaceful change when this seemed appropriate.

The king's dismissal of the Melbourne government in 1834 was to give a boost to the Conservative Party, and launch it on the road to recovery. As we have seen, it established Peel's supremacy over his colleagues and made him not only party leader but also prime minister. His government was in a minority, and consequently was only short-lived. After a series of parliamentary defeats, he asked the king to dissolve parliament and to hold an election in January 1835. For this, he took the opportunity to explain his new, milder Conservatism in an address to the voters.

c) The Tamworth Manifesto

Although Peel wrote the manifesto to his own constituents, he was really addressing the electorate at large. Copies of the seven-page document were sent to the London newspapers, and on publication there was an immediate reaction in the political world, where the manifesto caused 'a prodigious sensation'. In the past governments had occasionally listed their achievements in a document, but there had been nothing comparable to this declaration of principles on the eve of an election. As such, the Tamworth Manifesto was a publication without parallel, and its importance in establishing the tone of the Conservative Party was immense. Here was the basis for the new Conservatism, although neither the creed nor the party were mentioned by name. Peel asserted the need for strong government and the preservation of existing institutions, but combined this with an acceptance that the Reform Act was 'a final and irrevocable settlement of a great constitutional question'. He pledged a future Conservative government to review institutions without infringing on established rights, and to tackle proven abuses. He appealed to his earlier record as a minister to show that he had never supported the continuation of 'acknowledged evils', nor been 'the enemy of judicious reforms'. He wrote,

1 Then as to the spirit of the Reform Bill, and the willingness to
  adopt and enforce it as a rule of government. If by adopting the
  spirit of the Reform Bill it be meant that we are to live in a
  perpetual vortex of agitation - that public men can only support
5 themselves in public estimation by adopting every popular
  impression of the day, by promising the instant redress of anything
  which anybody may call an abuse, by abandoning altogether that
  great aid of government, more powerful than either law or reason,
  the respect for ancient rights, and the deference to prescriptive
10 authority; if this be the spirit of the Reform Bill, I will not
  undertake to adopt it; but if the spirit of the Reform Bill implies
  merely a careful review of institutions, civil and ecclesiastical,
  undertaken in a friendly temper, combining, with the firm
  maintenance of established rights, the correction of proved abuses,
15 and the redress of real grievances, in that case I can, for myself and
  my colleagues, undertake to act in such a spirit, and with such
  intentions.

This was a bold bid for the middle ground, at a time when party lines were less firmly delineated than they are today. Such attitudes were likely to strike a response in all those reasonable men who wanted effective government accompanied by judicious reform. It seemed a wise position to take, accepting the finality of what had been done without proceeding too rapidly along the road marked 'reform'. Landowners and *bourgeoisie* could unite in the defence of property, but by conceding the need for some further changes there was a likelihood of wider support. Gash neatly encapsulated the purpose of Peel's endeavour in his observation that the leader was 'trying to turn the Tory party of one particular class into the Conservative Party of the nation'.

However, the time was not yet ripe, and despite having begun to develop their organisation (see pages 69-70) the Conservatives were defeated in the election. The party improved its position, but was well short of a majority having won only 279 of the 658 seats. After several parliamentary defeats Peel resigned in April 1835.

d) Opposition, 1835-41

Peel quickly adjusted to the new situation, and stuck to his chosen path. He had no intention of allowing the Conservatives to revert to old Tory attitudes of narrow self-interest because he knew that they needed broader support in the community. But neither was he attracted to the strategy of seeking to outbid the Whigs by adopting a policy of bold reform in an attempt to win the support of radical opinion. At a time when the working classes lacked the vote, and neither party was interested in giving it to them, there was no electoral advantage to be gained from such a ploy. The times were too turbulent to make a widening of the franchise a realistic possibility, and Peel had no wish to consider it. He had no desire to ally with radicals within his own party or those outside. As he put it, 'My opinion is decidedly against all manoeuvres, all coquetting with radicalism for the mere purpose of a temporary triumph over the government'.

For Peel there was a middle way. This involved accepting the forces of change in society and coming to terms with them. It was really a similar policy of cautious reform to that which had been employed by Lord Liverpool in the 1820s, but which had come to an end when the Duke of Wellington became Prime Minister in 1828. After 1835 it was this path of creating a consensus of moderate opinion which Peel chose to follow. In line with this policy he developed the concept of responsible, non-partisan opposition. Not for him the approach of the Whig leader, Tierney, a decade earlier, who had asserted that, 'the task of the Opposition is to propose nothing, to oppose everything and to turn out the government'. Instead, Peel was prepared to support the Whig government whenever it behaved in what he believed to be a reasonable and just manner. He openly backed some of its reforms, even to the extent of saving the government from defeat. The Right doubted the wisdom of his approach, but it gave him more time to put the Conservative house in order and to convince the voters of his ability and capacity for leadership. Never before had there been such a responsible and well-prepared Opposition. The policy paid electoral dividends. Until 1867 general elections were held after the death of the monarch, and in 1837 the Conservatives further advanced their position in the election that followed William IV's death. They won a majority of the seats in England and Wales, but the Whigs were sustained in power by the strength of their support in Scotland and Ireland.

Peel's political skills were particularly apparent in the so-called Bedchamber Crisis of 1839. Melbourne resigned, and Queen Victoria reluctantly asked Peel to become Prime Minister. He requested the appointment of some Conservative ladies to serve in her bedchamber, rather than have her surrounded by the wives of Whig grandees. When she refused, Peel declined to take office. He felt that her attitude showed a lack of confidence in his leadership, and he would not compromise even though some of his supporters were impatient for another taste of power. Melbourne returned, and his ministry drifted on until in June 1841 Peel successfully put down a motion of 'No Confidence'. The government fell and in the general election which followed the Conservatives were victorious.

e) The 1841 Election

Peel won a decisive victory, gaining a majority of 76 seats. Radical attacks on vested interests had driven many landowners into the arms of the Conservatives. But above all, members of the landed interest warmed to the Conservative pledge to maintain the Corn Laws. Many Conservative candidates had adopted a highly protectionist position, despite the fact that Peel felt that trading policy was too complex an issue to be settled in an election campaign. Gains were made in every type of constituency and in all areas of the country, although it is clear that the Conservatives were strongest in the counties and in the small boroughs, rather than in the larger urban areas. Their greatest strength was in England, especially in the Midlands, and the south and east (outside of London). In Wales, Scotland, the north and south-west there was less of a swing away from the Whigs.

Many factors contributed to the Conservative success. The anti-reform stance of the Tories in 1831-2 had passed into memory, and there was some reaction against the Whigs who seemed to have been in office for a long time (11 years). Their handling of the national finances had been inept, and they were disunited. The Conservatives had responded to the growth of the electorate by developing their organisation around the country (see pages 69-70) and were in a position to maximise their support. However, that support owed much to the dominance of their leader, and was a striking indication of the regard many people had of his statesmanlike performance. No other politician was held in such high esteem, and as one contemporary put it, 'All turns on the name of Sir Robert Peel'.

The improvement in Conservative fortunes had been continuous since 1832, when they had been at the lowest point to which either of the two main parties fell in the nineteenth century. By 1841 they were in power. They had been much assisted by the unusual circumstance of three elections in the first nine years of the reformed parliament. This was the only time in the 35 years between the first two Reform Acts that a minority Opposition took office after a general election victory, and it was to be the only one in which the Conservatives were on the winning side. There was much relief in the country and in political circles that a strong government could now be formed. In 1841 the way seemed open to a new era of Conservative ascendancy.

Number of Conservatives returned in Elections during the 'Age of Peel'

	1832	1835	1837	1841
England (out of 471)	129	209	244	283
Scotland (.. .. 53)	10	15	20	22
Wales (.. .. 29)	13	17	18	19
Ireland (.. .. 105)	33	38	32	43
Total (.. .. 658)	185	279	314	367

---

f) Peel's Second Administration, 1841-6

Peel's Cabinet was an exceptionally impressive one, containing as it did five past or future prime ministers (in order, Lord Ripon (previously Lord Goderich), the Duke of Wellington, Peel himself, Lord Stanley and Lord Aberdeen) as well as other colleagues from previous governments. Its general character was predictable, for Peel gave office to many of the experienced men who had assisted him when the Conservatives were in opposition. The talented younger men - notably Gladstone, Herbert and Cardwell - were for the moment compelled to take a back seat, although Gladstone as Vice-President of the Board of Trade was to be deeply involved in devising and implementing Peel's free trading proposals. There was no room in the government for the ambitious Disraeli, who does not seem to have been seriously considered. As only a recent entrant to the House of Commons there was little reason why he should have been, but Disraeli felt resentful about his omission. His 'rebuff' was eventually to drive him into the ranks of the malcontents on the backbenches, and Peel was to pay a heavy price for Disraeli's wounded pride.

g) Peel's Concept of the Premiership

Peel's own authority was unchallenged. He had an unrivalled national reputation and was indispensable to the fortunes of the Conservative Party. His intellectual pre-eminence and his strategic vision gave him a dominance over his colleagues and as Prime Minister he had a clear sense of purpose and relentlessly drove his colleagues in the direction in which he wished to go. Government had a coherence which had long been lacking, and from the beginnings the ministry was clearly embarked upon a mainly constructive path. Peel's rather aloof manner did not invite discussion. He was rather autocratic, and exercised an unusual amount of day-to-day control over the entire administration. He was very well-informed about all aspects of policy, and had a masterly grasp of detail. Colleagues recognised how conscientiously he carried out his duties and were mostly willing to accept the lead he gave them. As Sir James Graham, the Home Secretary, explained, 'We never had a minister who was so truly a first minister as he is. He makes himself felt in every department, and is really cognisant of the affairs of each'.

Although his colleagues were an unusually able group of men, Peel wished to be fully informed about every aspect of policy. As far as he was concerned responsibility ultimately lay with him, and so he took on a burden of work which was quite exceptional. He even introduced his own budgets, and Gladstone noted that government was not so much conducted by the Cabinet, as by the heads of department in individual consultation with the Prime Minister. It was this personal control which led to the allegation that the ministry was no more than a 'Cabinet of Peel's dolls'. No Prime Minister has subsequently so dominated the process of administration, and the growth in the scope and complexity of modern government business make it impossible for it to happen again. However, it is a tribute to Peel's performance that, when Ramsay MacDonald became the first Labour Prime Minister in 1924, he was presented with a set of the Peel Papers as the best guide to the role of Premier.

h) Financial and Social Reform

On taking over, Peel wanted to do something to improve the lot of the 'labouring classes of society'. He was appalled by the hunger and misery around the country, which was particularly severe in some areas. Britain had become increasingly urbanised, and the birth-pangs of an industrialising society were associated with a series of appalling social conditions in the towns and cities which led to popular discontent. Peel was concerned at the threat of disorder that this situation posed, because he believed that it was essential to maintain social stability. Graham shared Peel's worries and was determined that any lawlessness should be quickly tackled, whether it came from Irish agitators, from Chartists, or from elsewhere. Alarmed at the excesses of working-class agitators, he urged magistrates 'to act with vigour and without parley'. He was nervous about mob rule and was anxious to see large public meetings suppressed.

Tory backbenchers had no reason to complain about any lack of resolution on the government's part when it was faced with matters of law and order. Yet such resolve was combined with reforming measures to ease social distress, and Peel felt that improvements in the level of general prosperity were necessary. This is not the place for a detailed critique of the work of his reforming ministry, but its achievements merit some explanation and indicate some of the strengths and deficiencies of the Peelite approach to public affairs.

When Peel took office in 1841 the national finances were in a parlous state. Bereft of ideas, the Whigs had allowed the situation to drift, and five years of regular annual deficits had culminated in a total of the then huge sum of £2m. Peel took personal responsibility for the direction of affairs. He wanted to expand the economy and he lost no time in changing the thrust of government policy. The effect of his innovatory budgets was to liberalise trade by removing or reducing a large number of customs duties. To make up for the immediate loss of revenue he boldly reintroduced Income Tax, a tax on income from land which previously had only been levied in war-time. He explained his decision in the Budget speech of 1842.

1 It is my duty to make an appeal to the possessors of property ... I
   propose that the income of this country should bear a charge not
   exceeding 7d in the pound; for the purpose of not only supplying
   the deficiency in the revenue, but of enabling me to propose great
5 commercial reforms, which will afford a hope of reviving
   commerce, and, by diminishing the prices of the articles of
   consumption, and the cost of living, will compensate you for your
   present sacrifices.

Although he was not a doctrinaire Free Trader, he became convinced of the need for tariff reductions. He hoped that they would lower prices and expand consumption to create a new prosperity from which all classes in the community would benefit. This would strike at the root cause of social distress, and bring about a general improvement in the standard of living. Some of his backbenchers feared that the government's adoption of free trade in one area meant that sooner or later it would be applied agriculture; they feared that the survival of the Corn Laws would be short-lived.

Other measures were introduced to strengthen the financial system. The Bank Charter Act of 1844 brought about much tighter control over the banking system. It increased the power of the Bank of England over note-issue, and placed greater controls over private banks. By so doing it paved the way for the eventual supremacy of the Bank of England and the structure Peel created lasted well into the twentieth century. As Briggs has noted, 'Although effective central bank management and techniques took years to evolve, the Victorians could look back to Peel as the architect of a confident economic order'.

The thinking behind the Companies Act, also of 1844, was not dissimilar. It set out to remove irregularities which a parliamentary committee had identified in 1844: 'For years, the world [has] been at the mercy of anyone who chose to publish an advertisement, call himself a company, and receive money for assurances and annuities'. The Act sought to increase public and commercial confidence in the reliability of businesses, by insisting that they should be registered and produce annual accounts. Like the Bank Charter Act, the Companies Act was concerned to end what Peel regarded as 'reckless speculation' and to ensure that business and commerce were put on a sounder footing.

In the area of social reform, Peel did little and what was offered was mainly in response to public pressure or as a result of the campaigning of committed individuals. The Mines Act of 1842 forbade the employment of women and young children underground, after the revelations of a Royal Commission had shocked public opinion. Graham's Factory Act reduced the hours which could be worked by women and children under 13, and with its requirement for the fencing of machinery it was a useful advance. Yet in both cases, it was the work of the philanthropic Lord Ashley (later Lord Shaftesbury) which drew the matter to government attention and provided the impetus for improvement. Peel and Graham were sceptical about the value of direct measures of social reform, regarding them as at best palliatives, and at worst a serious limitation on the freedom of manufacturers to run their enterprises as efficiently as possible. They believed that it was not the state's role to produce legislation to tackle social discontent. It was more important to ensure that there was plenty of employment and cheap bread available. Their view was that only by improving the purchasing power of the masses could the condition of the people be transformed.

i) Ireland

In 1841 disorder in Ireland was growing and many Irishmen were agitating for a repeal of the Act of Union between Britain and Ireland. Daniel O'Connell, the hero of the struggle for Catholic Emancipation, led the moderate movement which urged the need for change, but his leadership of the Irish cause was being challenged by a new generation of nationalists who were discontented with his lack of revolutionary fervour. Many of the firebrands were to be found in the 'Young Ireland' movement which was prepared to resort to force to achieve its aims. When O'Connell began to address a series of mass meetings which clamoured for repeal, the strength of his movement could no longer be ignored. The government was under pressure from *The Times*, the Duke of Wellington, and Irish Protestant peers to act firmly by clamping down on all agitation. A vast meeting to be held in Clontarf was banned and

O'Connell was arrested, convicted and imprisoned. He was discredited, and the government's more hard-line supporters were relieved.

Although he was a firm believer in law and order, Peel wished to be constructive, and much of his Irish policy showed a liberality of outlook which was rare at the time. He was one of the few Conservatives of the nineteenth century to have any understanding of Irish issues, and was convinced that, 'Mere force, however necessary the application of it, will do nothing as a permanent remedy for the social evils of that country'. His aim was to gain the sympathy of wealthy and intelligent Roman Catholics in support of the Union, so that men of property in both Britain and Ireland could work together, irrespective of religious differences. If he was to achieve this goal, the grievances of the Catholic population needed to be addressed, for Peel appreciated 'the necessity of disuniting, by the legitimate means of a just, kind and conciliatory policy, the Roman Catholic body, and thus breaking up a sullen and formidable confederacy against the British connection'.

In its more conciliatory phase, the government hoped to win approval by a series of initiatives. An attempt at franchise reform met with opposition on the Tory Right, and Peel's attempts at tackling the thorny issue of land tenure met with a similar fate. He had established a Commission into agrarian problems, particularly those concerning land law, and when Lord Devon's committee reported, Peel put forward a Bill to allow for limited compensation to those tenants who carried out improvements. However, he was unable to carry it through the Lords because of opposition from hard-line peers and Irish landowners, and the proposal was withdrawn.

Peel also wanted the Catholic population to be given the chance to take up official positions, and this required the development of more educational opportunities. He was particularly keen to promote opportunities for the joint education of Protestants and Catholics, for he wanted to break down barriers between the two religious communities. However, this non-sectarian approach aroused great controversy. Peel wanted to see three new Queen's Colleges established to educate Irishmen irrespective of their religious creed, a proposal which was opposed by both Anglicans, who thought it ungodly, and Catholics, who wanted nothing to do with them.

More controversially, he wished to develop Maynooth College, Dublin, a Catholic seminary. In April 1845, the government offered £30,000 for rebuilding, and wished to increase the annual grant, in a bid to appease the Catholic clergy. To his credit, Peel pressed ahead with the proposal even though it was unpopular on all sides. Catholics were unimpressed and many of his Protestant supporters in the Commons were deeply affronted. They felt that Peel was striking a blow against one of the foundations of their Tory philosophy, namely support for the Anglican cause. Party unity was seriously strained and 149 backbenchers voted against the measure. Hostile petitions flooded in to

Downing Street, a National Club 'in support of the Protestant principles of the Constitution' was established as a breakaway from the Carlton Club, and Lord Ashley led a Protestant Association committed to the repeal of the Act. Peel's popularity within the Conservative party was at a low ebb.

As the controversy raged, the issue at the heart of it came to matter less than did the personal honour of the Prime Minister. For many Tories Peel's behaviour revived old suspicions. One compared him to Judas Iscariot, and commented that 'as Sir Robert Peel betrayed the Protestant Church in 1829, so he is going to betray the Protestant Church in Ireland in 1845. I can have no confidence in a man who obtained office by fraud, and who dares to trample underfoot the best interests of the country'.

Punch expressed something of their contempt in its refrain;

> 'How wonderful is Peel
> He changeth with the Time,
> Turning and twisting like an eel
> Ascending through the slime'.

As well as placing further strain on party loyalty in general, the Maynooth question severed most of the remaining bonds between Peel and the Tory Right. For the moment his position was secure as there was no-one in a position to mount a challenge. However, the Irish potato famine was an even more sensitive issue, and it was shortly to provide the supreme crisis in Peel's career.

j) The Corn Laws

In the 1841 election the almost clean sweep the Conservatives had made in the county constituencies had depended on the pledge to maintain the Corn Laws. However, agricultural protection was never a matter of absolute principle for the Conservative leader, and he was willing to consider modifications to the existing arrangements. In 1842 he revised the sliding scale of duties which had been adopted in 1828, and soon afterwards he concluded that the Corn Laws should be repealed when the time was right. In his considerations he was influenced by the propaganda of the Anti-Corn Law League which argued for free trade and stressed that the effect of the Laws was to keep the price of bread artificially high. As we have seen, he was worried about the threat to public order, especially as high food prices were a cause of distress in 1842, when there was widespread Chartist activity.

By 1845 agriculture was in a privileged position as the only area of economic activity still substantially protected by tariffs against competing imports. Having examined corn prices at home and abroad, Peel concluded that this protection, in the form of the Corn Laws, was not necessary to assist the agricultural interest. He felt that the landowners' prosperity depended on efficiency and a strong home market, rather than any artificial barriers to trade. Therefore, he concluded, they did not need the retention of the Corn Laws. He was also convinced that, if the Laws were removed and grain was made more cheaply available, lower bread prices would not encourage manufacturers to reduce workers' wage levels. Careful analysis had persuaded him that wages did not vary with the price of corn. For instance, wages were relatively high in 1843 when bread prices were untypically low.

However, Peel's motives were more political than economic, for he knew that the Corn Laws were a cause of resentment, and that their removal would help to guarantee stability and order. They were seen by many people as a symbol of an outmoded past in which the aristocracy had possessed great privilege, and the middle and working classes had been denied a share of power. They were a reminder of the dark days after 1815 when an unpopular government had seemed to be acting in the interests of its own supporters only. As one contemporary observed, 'the Corn Laws are considered a class monopoly, and are thus most detrimental to aristocratic and to the landed interest'.

Peel's private thoughts on the inevitability and desirability of repeal were shared with only a few very close colleagues. He realised that many Tories in the House of Commons had a different outlook. They firmly believed in the protection of corn, and were already suspicious about his commitment to their point of view. His own Chancellor, Goulburn, gave him a warning in 1845 that,

1 An abandonment of your former opinions now would, I think, prejudice your character as a public man ... In my opinion, the party of which you are the head is the only barrier which remains against the revolutionary effects of the Reform Bill. If it be broken
5 in pieces by a destruction of confidence in its leaders (and I cannot but think that an abandonment of the Corn Law would produce that result), I see nothing before us but class animosities and the ultimate triumph of unrestrained democracy.

Within Peel's Cabinet there were serious differences of opinion and at first only three ministers supported him. However, such was his authority and so relentless his power of argument, that he won over the bulk of the others to his viewpoint. In the words of Norman Gash, 'the debate seemed to revolve for the most part around the time, mode, justification and responsibility of abandoning them [the Corn Laws]'.

In party terms, the Cabinet was not Peel's main problem. He was aware of the deep distrust of his intentions on the backbenches. He hoped that he would be able to let the parliament run its course and then fight the next election on the issue of free trade in corn. In that way he would not be so vulnerable to the charge of betrayal of the agricultural interest. Everything depended on the harvest, and as Gladstone remarked, 'one bad harvest, or at all events two, would break up the Corn Laws with the party ... it is a law mainly dependent on the weather'. The summer of 1845 was wet, and potato blight spread to the British Isles from continental Europe. In parts of England this meant

THE RISING GENERATION—IN PARLIAMENT.

Peel. "WELL, MY LITTLE MAN, WHAT ARE YOU GOING TO DO THIS SESSION, EH?"

D——li (the Juvenile). "WHY—AW—AW—I'VE MADE ARRANGEMENTS—AW—TO SMASH—AW—EVERYBODY."

'The Rising Generation', Punch *cartoon, January 1847*

hunger: in parts of Ireland it led to widespread starvation. Peel believed that something had to be done, for the sake of the working classes in Britain as in Ireland. In itself, repeal would not do much for the Irish peasantry who could not afford to buy bread but it would help protect British labourers from high bread prices in times of scarcity. Peel seized the opportunity to announce the suspension of the Corn Laws and the impossibility of reintroducing them.

k) Opposition to Repeal

His action was a challenge to the fundamental beliefs of many Conservatives. Peel was now seen as the arch-traitor who had again let the party's supporters down on a major issue. Disraeli, disappointed at his lack of advancement, now had an opportunity to exploit the revolt to further his own career. He taunted Peel mercilessly and articulated the bitterness of the agriculturalists who saw protection as vital to their interests. Lord George Bentinck was their spokesman, and his backing made it possible for Disraeli to gather in their support. Bentinck wielded the sledge-hammer and Disraeli employed the more deadly rapier.

Until this controversy Bentinck had rarely spoken in the House of Commons. Politics had never been his consuming passion. He was more interested in breeding and racing horses, and was a well-known, if controversial, figure on the turf where he was involved in several rows and duels. His main claim to national fame had been in 1844 when he had been prominent in exposing a fraud surrounding the Derby. As a country landowner and heir to a vast estate, he represented the sort of dilettante approach to politics which Peel despised. Yet Bentinck was no Ultra. In earlier times he had been Private Secretary to Canning, had supported the Whigs over reform in 1830, and had been offered a position by Peel in his Second Administration. Unlike many on the Right he had actually backed Peel over the Maynooth Grant.

It was the proposal to repeal the Corn Laws which aroused him to fury. He had never been closely associated with Disraeli, but between them 'the Jockey and the Jew' mounted a formidable assault on the Peelite leadership. Bentinck had none of Disraeli's subtlety or flair. He was much more given to extravagant and even violent language, and in 1845-6 he turned his biting invective on the leader whom he thought had betrayed his party. He was no orator, but his contemptuous manner made him effective in a brutal sort of way. He represented the raw anger of the agricultural lobby against a man whom they regarded as dishonourable, even treacherous. He reckoned that in bygone days the reprisals for Peel's behaviour would have been severe - 'I believe the punishment in the good old days for offences of this kind used to be cropping the ears and putting the vagabonds in the pillory'.

Early on, Disraeli made the comparison of Protectionism in 1845 and the Protestant cause in 1828-9, and, after accusing him of tampering 'with the generous confidence of a great people and a great party', he went on to savage Peel at his most vulnerable point.

> Dissolve if you please the parliament you have betrayed and appeal to the people who, I believe, mistrust you. For me, there remains this at least - the opportunity of expressing publicly my belief that a Conservative government is an organized hypocrisy.

Peel found the invective difficult to answer. He believed that he was acting rightly and consistently and in the interests of the whole community. Such was the situation that repeal was necessary, and as the queen's minister he must have the flexibility to act as he felt appropriate. If necessary he was prepared to disrupt his party in the struggle, and he was consoled by the belief that,

> If I fall, I shall have the satisfaction of reflecting that I do not fall because I have shown subservience to a party ... and preferred the interests of a party to the general right of the community.

1) Protectionism in the Conservative Party

Among the Conservative protectionists there was much suspicion of the government's policies. There was also a personal element in their opposition. Bentinck had not forgiven Peel for failing to serve in Canning's government in 1827, and Disraeli felt that his talents as a parliamentarian had not been sufficiently recognised. Neither had ever found Peel personally congenial. Yet both had been supporters of his administration in the early years, and Disraeli only became very disillusioned as the lack of emphasis on traditional Tory values became apparent. Others in the Party were also increasingly uneasy at the Peelite approach to Conservatism, its tone and its direction. They thought that it placed too much emphasis on a moderate and consensual style, and too little on the old Tory principles. They watched Peel with growing anxiety and mistrust.

For many of them the repeal of the Corn Laws was the last straw. As landowners, they took it for granted that agriculture was at the heart of the country's prosperity. They thought that its protection from foreign competition was essential both to the nation and to the social and economic position of the aristocracy in the community. They believed that an abandonment of the Corn Laws would put their status and influence at risk, and they had no wish to see this imperilled at the behest of the manufacturers of the Anti-Corn Law League, who had been clamouring for repeal. The League felt that the Corn Laws symbolised the unjust predominance of agriculture over manufacturing , and that this was unacceptable. Many protectionists were determined to cling on to that privileged position, and particularly disliked the thought of a

Conservative Prime Minister bowing to the pressure of the industrialists. The Corn Laws were seen by them as representing their last security against ruin, and they expected a Conservative government to retain them. It was assumed that the Party leader would defend, not undermine, the landed classes and their way of life. In this they were reflecting the unmistakable feeling of the whole agrarian community, for the campaigning of the farmers in 1845-6 was intensive.

Tenant farmers as a group lacked direct representation in the House of Commons, but they lobbied the landowners who were there, both individually and via the local Protection Societies they had formed. They were determined that there should be 'No Surrender' over the Corn Laws. They urged Conservative MPs to defend the agricultural cause on the basis that the Party was the voice of the countryside. At first some landowners were hesitant about a challenge to Peel for they knew that the issue would be a divisive and damaging one, but their resolve was strengthened by this local pressure. The protectionists proceeded to act in parliament as a powerful 'third force', with their own unofficial leadership, organisation and national backing, and, as the Corn crisis unfolded, control of the Party gradually slipped out of Peel's grasp.

Although not all of the Conservative landowners opposed Peel, the bulk of them were hostile. In the final vote on repeal only 112 Conservatives supported him, while 241 voted against - the measure was only passed with Whig support. The scale of the revolt was greater than that over the Maynooth Grant, although the majority of those who opposed Peel then opposed him again in 1846. The strongest antagonism came from those MPs who represented rural areas, and even a few who were personally free traders joined with the protectionists in the parliamentary divisions. They bowed to the pressure of local feeling. Gash's research indicates that 86 per cent of Conservative MPs representing the countryside rejected repeal, whilst of those who sat for larger boroughs only 54 per cent did so. Clearly, much depended on the type of constituency MPs represented.

m) Peel's handling of the Issue

Following the passage of the act repealing the corn laws many of the landed gentry were furious at Peel and they helped to bring about the defeat of the government on a bill to strengthen its powers in dealing with violence in Ireland. Whigs and protectionists combined against him, and Peel resigned in June 1846. The Conservative Party was now fundamentally split between the influential group of young men who saw Peel as their guide and mentor, and the protectionists among whom Disraeli had acquired considerable standing.

For Peel, good government was at stake, and repeal, as he later told his Tamworth constituents, tended to fortify the established institutions of the country, to inspire confidence in the equity and benevolence of the legislature, and to discourage the desire for further reform in the constitution of the House of Commons. As such it was a highly conservative measure and, like the 1832 Reform Act, the removal of just that sort of grievance which, untackled, leads to revolution. He had a good case from the point of view of a far-sighted conservative who wanted to defend the conservative cause, but from the point of view of the Conservative Party and its major supporters the repeal was a devastating blow.

Robert Blake, a leading authority on the Conservative Party, has claimed that Peel's decision was sound enough, but that in his handling of the issue he was maladroit; 'It was Peel's merit as a statesman that he normally adapted his policies to the need for change. It was his deficit as a politician that he did so in a manner which, combining as it did, prickliness, egotism, self-exculpation and unctuousness, gave a formidable handle to his enemies'.

Certainly, Peel's personality was an important factor in the break-up of the party. That schism was itself the culmination of a series of skirmishes between the leader and those whose support he needed to retain. By his actions, and the manner in which he went about them, he bears a responsibility for wrecking the party he had done so much to create. To Blake, it is, therefore, really from 1846 and not 1835 that modern Conservatism should be dated. For whilst Peel was in the wilderness, Disraeli and Bentinck lived to fight another day. The modern party emerged out of the confusion of the Corn Law conflict.

3 Organisational Matters

The Conservatives were the first of the national parties to begin to organise. In the year of the Reform Act the Carlton Club was established as the new party headquarters. By the end of the decade the party was being run on the basis of an alliance between leader, Chief Whip and the Principal Agent. There was never a complete division of labour but broadly the leader and the Chief Whip were responsible for parliamentary matters, and the Conservative Election Committee, including the Chief Whip and Agent, looked after affairs outside the Lords and the Commons.

a) At Westminster

The period between 1832 and 1867 is often referred to as the 'golden age of the private member'. Parliamentary patronage had declined as a means of retaining the loyalty of MPs. Fewer of them were beholden either to royal influence or to the landowners who had controlled so many pocket boroughs. Sixty-five of the most notorious of these had been removed, and the influence of their proprietors over the composition of the House of Commons had been accordingly reduced. As yet, the heavy hand of modern party discipline had not appeared, and strong whipping was not usually in evidence. In this situation, MPs cherished their independence of action, and were not easily persuaded to vote according to the party line. In 1832 there was no reliable means of deciding the party affiliation of every MP, for in the words of Professor Gash, 'party membership was not at that time an intelligible expression'. Particularly in the Conservative Party there was a mood of fractious disarray after its election debacle, and there was a need for some attempt to manage the House and to tighten up on matters of discipline.

The Whips mustered as much support as possible and tried to keep ministers in touch with backbenchers. They could hold out the hope of future ministerial office should the party seem likely to win the next election. But this was not enough for Peel. He was concerned at the unpredictability of the Conservative vote in the House of Commons. Knowing that the new and tighter discipline was unlikely to be appreciated, he saw the need to achieve a better rapport with the rank and file. He addressed gatherings of the whole parliamentary party to explain some plan or policy and to plead for better attendance. In addition, he occasionally met its leading members at his Drayton home to discuss tactics and ideas, and by such approaches he imparted a sense of direction to the Conservative Party. However, for all his efforts, the 'tightening up' of parliamentary behaviour did not go unchallenged, and some MPs found it irksome. Relations with them were continually under strain.

b) The Carlton Club

The link between the party leadership and local Conservative 'notables' in the country was provided via the Carlton Club - in the same way that the Reform Club acted for the Whigs. It was explicitly political in purpose, providing a social centre for party members in both Houses and influential supporters in the provinces, as well as a home for party management and organisation. The Whips had offices there, and with the aid of the Principal Agent they kept in touch with the constituencies, collecting information, bringing candidates and constituencies together, and maintaining contact with local associations and agents.

F.R. Bonham was the Principal Agent during the time that Sir Robert Peel led the party. He was highly competent and he served his leader well. The two men were personal friends, and Bonham frequently met Peel to keep him informed of party feeling. Bonham's talent in running campaigns was evident in the 1835 general election, and soon afterwards he suggested to Peel that a small, permanent Election Committee should be set up to ensure a more organised and professional direction of local activity. This was done, and under the chairmanship of Lord

Granville Somerset, it supervised elections, helping in the raising of money and the selection of candidates, as well as collecting information on the registration of voters in the constituencies.

From his base in the Carlton Club, Bonham was thus able to reorganise the party, and mobilise Conservative feeling in the country where he was instrumental in encouraging the formation of a network of Conservative Associations. He was also concerned with party finance, for from 1835 there existed a central party fund under the trusteeship of Wellington and Peel. Bonham was involved in the dispersal of funds to suitable and needy candidates, such as Disraeli.

c) Outside Westminster

In 1830 party organisation outside parliament was still almost non-existent in many places. Only 2 per cent of the population had the vote, and each MP represented on average only about 330 voters. Some represented hardly any at all. It was the expansion of the electorate which changed the situation, for once the number of voters increased, the outcome of elections was more uncertain. Parties had to consider ways of organising support among these newly-enfranchised electors, and their attempts to do so mark the beginnings of the modern party system.

This was all the more important because of a minor requirement of the Reform Act, by which a person's name needed to be placed on the electoral register and a small fee paid before he could vote. This was not always easy, especially where an illiterate person had to establish his voting qualification. Both Whigs and Conservatives established Registration Societies after 1832 to see that potential voters were placed on the electoral list. Sometimes they were set up by local notables, sometimes by candidates, and sometimes at the behest of the parliamentary Whips. Membership was small, as in the early 1830s half of the borough constituencies had less than 2000 voters. Within these Registration Societies activists became adept at ensuring that likely party supporters were on the voting roll, and that the names of likely opponents were removed. As such, they were more often agencies of corruption than well-organised and disciplined organisations. Yet they represented an early form of election machinery, and demonstrated the way in which voters could be organised and directed. Their activities were co-ordinated by the London headquarters at the Carlton Club, which took a close interest in the state of local registration and party strength. Peel saw the importance of the development and in 1837 urged his supporters to 'register, register, register'. The effort was successful. By 1841 Conservative organisation nationally and locally was impressively developed.

4 Assessment of the Peelite Contribution

In 1850, four years after his fall from office, Peel died as the result of a riding accident. For years his reputation had been almost unchallenged in the country, and he enjoyed immense popularity. On his death large numbers of working men sent in their pennies to pay for statues in his memory, and the scores of them erected in the industrial towns of the north reveal him to the nation as a Victorian hero - a fine example of the gospel of hard work. Eulogies abounded, and *The Times* obituary noted that 'Peel has been our chief guide from the confusions and darkness that hung around the beginning of the century to the comparatively quiet haven in which we are now embayed'.

That he dominated early-Victorian politics is a commonplace and few would deny that he was a highly capable statesman. He has had a good press both in his own time and subsequently. Bagehot was simultaneously drawn to and repelled by him, but acknowledged him to be a fitting man for his times, and above all 'a great administrator'. Disraeli observed that 'he was a transcendent administrator of public business and a matchless master of debate in a popular assembly'.

More recently, Lord (formerly R.A.) Butler, a moderate (post-war) Conservative thinker and politician, saw himself as a follower of Peel. As a believer in practical reform , he admired Peel as an exponent of 'the art of the possible'. He admired his early work at the Home Office, where he demonstrated a firm approach, but combined this with a policy of reform. Of the later period, Butler felt that Peel had been in error over the 1832 Reform Act, but admired the way in which he adjusted to its consequences and proceeded to 'build [our] modern creed'. He related that when he and his colleagues were attempting to restate Conservative principles after 1945 they used the Tamworth Manifesto as their starting-point.

A significant amount of the more academic writing about Peel has been contributed by Asa Briggs, for whom his administrative pre-eminence, his industry and his sense of responsibility were praiseworthy qualities, as were the thoroughness of his grasp of detail and his capacity to take decisions. He believes that between 1841 and 1846 Peel's finest qualities were revealed; he 'impressed his personality and outlook on his well-balanced cabinet with exceptional force'. But probably the historian who has written most prolifically on Peel has been Professor Norman Gash. He has produced numerous articles and books from a sympathetic standpoint. These present a picture of Peel as the architect of the mid-Victorian era of stability and prosperity which, sadly, he did not live to see. In particular, Gash commends Peel's response to the issue of the Corn Laws, which 'did more than anything else to heal the social breach and restore the confidence in a political system that was still aristocratic and oligarchic'.

A refreshing analysis has been provided by Bruce Coleman. In his study *Conservatism and the Conservative Party in Nineteenth Century Britain* he has looked at the party from a more sceptical viewpoint. Stressing its defensive reaction to an often threatening world, he sees its fundamental purposes being to prevent change and to defend the self-interest of the men of property. He is unconvinced by much of the analysis of Conservatism, for he detects that, 'The party's most familiar figures were being elevated not just to the Pantheon of the Good, but also to the Pantheon of the Progressive'. None of them were portrayed as solid Tories, but rather as Liberal Conservatives, Peel and Disraeli being 'the most conspicuous beneficiaries of this tendency'. He believes that many studies have been written by sympathetic historians who were keen to present a 'sanitised version', or by post-war writers who were personally liberal progressives and who wished to believe that such men as Peel and Disraeli were of a similar persuasion. By contrast, Coleman views Conservatives as people who wished to 'stem change, not to encourage it', and observes that many possessed an evident distaste for much of what the nineteenth century had brought them.

Such an approach stresses the essential cautiousness of Conservatism, and in Peel's case it is worth remembering that he suffered from a degree of nervousness about social disorder which was unusual even among Tory politicians. Twice, in 1831-2 and 1842, he sent ammunition down from London, and fortified Drayton Manor to defend it against rioters from the neighbouring industrial districts. His insistence that the government must move quickly to stabilise the constitution was clearly influenced by his fears for life, family and property.

Coleman's views are helpful in reminding us of the limitations of Peel's more enlightened Conservatism. The stern defender of Peterloo and the Six Acts was later a firm opponent of the extension of the franchise, and though Peel is often portrayed as the man who was willing to introduce necessary reform, it was often an acceptance of change he could not easily avoid. He opposed several constructive measures of the time until their passage became inevitable, 'his perception of necessary action came, almost invariably, at the eleventh hour'. Of his great achievements, most were significantly by way of 'repeal'. He knew how to clear the ground, but was not the man to build upon it. Most of the legislation he was responsible for derived not from his own thinking, but from the suggestions of others, and when he took them up they were a commonplace of social thought. The prospect of change was in many ways abhorrent to him, yet it is surely to his credit that when convinced of the need to act, he was willing to translate other people's ideas into concrete action. He knew when to give way, and did not shirk from the challenge, however unpopular it might be.

Coleman recognised that there was an element of fear in Peel's approach to reform.

1 The experiences of 1828-32 seem to have convinced Peel that issues which jeopardised political and social order should be settled when the opportunity offered. "Letting sleeping dogs lie" was too dangerous. Better to anticipate inevitable change, so that
5 the terms of adjustment were controlled by the "friends of order" rather than dictated to them by opponents. His reactions may have put strains on his supporters, but they shared his firm resistance to agitation and radicalism.

a) Peel and the Conservative Party

For some Conservatives Peel is an unsatisfactory figure, and it is significant that references to him in party literature are often cursory and not wholly flattering. This is not altogther surprising for he gave a lower priority to party unity than any of his successors have dared to do. If he can be credited with the refashioning of the Conservative Party in the 1830s, so he must share some of the blame for its schism in 1846. He always placed much strain on the loyalty of his followers, and was unable or unwilling to woo them round to his viewpoint. Sometimes, his manner seemed to exacerbate their antagonism.

In a speech delivered in Tamworth to mark the 150th anniversary of the publication of the Manifesto, Leon Brittain, a Home Secretary of the early-Thatcher era in the 1980s, reassessed Peel's work. Noting that the Tamworth Manifesto marked 'the beginnings of the modern Conservative Party', he contrasted the fortunes of Peel and Disraeli in party mythology. The one was solidly northern, solidly commercial and in spirit solidly middle-class, and 'lacked that elusive magic from which golden myths are spun'. By contrast, Disraeli had flair. His memory was perpetuated soon after his death by the formation of the Primrose League, and subsequently by countless Tories anxious to place themselves in the Tory tradition. Indeed, at the annual party conference, it is rare for no one to seek to invoke the Disraelian spirit. As Brittain notes, 'Conservative politicians daily jostle to claim some part of the legacy of Peel's great enemy and successor, that brilliant showman, Disraeli'. His words are quoted, re-quoted and frequently misquoted, 'but no primrose blooms for Peel'. Yet this was the man who towered over his contemporaries on the political stage, and Brittain stresses that the Tamworth Manifesto signalled a new Conservative attitude to reform. Indeed, he was keen to associate the Thatcher government of the 1980s with his policies, with its emphasis on economic liberalism to create prosperity, on an appeal to the solid middle class and on the blessings of the alleged 'trickle down' effect to the mass of the population.

Of course, one reason for the down-playing of Peel in the party's history is that he placed less emphasis on the traditional Tory principles which he is often accused of betraying. For the partisan, anxious to see the purity of party principle preserved, Peel is a suspect figure. Those who adapt principles to the demands of the moment are open to such a charge, the more so if they were once among the most vociferous in defending them. Yet moderates such as Lord Butler, and many others in the modern party, would feel that his willingness to make concessions and his ability to recognise the best time to give way are good reasons to admire him.

In the early 1970s another Conservative leader and Prime Minister, Edward Heath, was to face similar difficulties with the Tory Right when he reversed a number of policies which he had espoused in the 1970 election. The charge used against him was that he was going in for 'U-turns'. Or was he realistically adapting, compromising, recognising the needs of the moment? To go on pursuing a theory which manifestly seems no longer applicable, would surely be against the national interests.

Peel could be said to be the pioneer of the political U-turn. He faced the dilemma of many statesmen. Were the interests that the party served best protected by an implacable resistance to the forces of change, or by a policy of tactical concession to the inevitable? Should prudent Conservatives seek to confront agitation, or to placate it with a show of moderation and legislative activity? Peel's instincts were for prudent concession at a safe moment. On certain issues it might be wiser to concede in good time and gain the credit, rather than to suffer humiliation at a later date. He saw the inevitability of change before others in the party, and knew when to give way. He met with the entrenched opposition of many Conservatives, and his relations with the party were inevitably strained. Ultimately, he failed to convince enough of its supporters of the merits of his form of Conservatism, and many of them particularly disliked the way in which he was often yielding to precisely those forces which he had hitherto spent so much time resisting.

b) Party versus Nation

For Disraeli, party loyalty was the prime consideration, and he scorned the policy of graduated concession which in his novel *Coningsby,* he derided as 'Tory men and Whig measures'. He believed that men should 'stand by the principles by which they rise, be they right or wrong'. His greatest eminence was to come in the very different electoral conditions after 1867, and in a sense his voice is nearer to that of the twentieth century, 'Above all, maintain the line of demarcation between parties, for it is only by maintaining the independence of party that you can maintain the integrity of public men, and the power and influence of Parliament itself'. His apologia for party looked to the future, whilst Peel's defence of his actions looked to the past.

On two great occasions Peel changed his mind and felt compelled to act. In 1829 and again in 1846 he believed that he was placing the well-being of the nation before all lesser considerations. He still thought in terms of the traditional standards expected of a minister of the Crown - that he should do his best to ensure just, efficient and stable rule, and that the monarch's government was carried on. In this way he was not a party politician in the modern sense of the term, and he did not hesitate to put the claims of duty and conscience first.

In saying that he was placing the interests of the country before his party, he had a good case. It would have been a better one if he had taken more time and trouble to make his followers aware of the reasons for his change of mind. Furthermore, it is a difficulty of his position that he was once associated with one set of policies, and then took over those of his opponents. If leaders do this whenever the national situation appears to require a reversal, it is not surprising if they stand accused of opportunism. Followers support their party leaders on the basis of established expectations, and it must undermine confidence in the standards of public life if they find that those expectations have been abandoned - even more so, if they are not fully in the picture as to why the change is considered necessary.

Many would see Peel as the creator of the modern Conservative Party, in that he moulded it into a national, pragmatic and unideological party above sectional interests, and based upon the Tamworth Manifesto. If his career had stopped in 1841, when back in office with a large majority, his reputation as a Conservative would stand high. He had steered the party through many difficult times and had made it stronger and more efficient than it had ever been before. The difficulty was that after 1841 he had less time to spend on the party, and his inevitable neglect meant that tensions which were always present widened throughout his second ministry. In the end, he helped to split the movement he had so laboriously built up.

c) Peel's Legacy to Nineteenth-Century Liberalism

Peel did carry with him into the wilderness the support of many of the 'officers' of the party, even if he lost that of many of the 'troops'. The pro-Peelite Conservatives gave him their loyalty and continued to follow him personally whilst he was alive. They were men of substance, among the most able administrators of the time, and Lord Rosebery later wrote that, 'To be a Peelite was a distinction in itself; it denoted statesmanship, industry and conscience'.

Rosebery was himself a Liberal Prime Minister of the late-nineteenth century, and the impact of Peel on late-Victorian Liberalism was considerable. Leading figures such as Gladstone and Cardwell eventually moved into the Liberal camp, and coloured its outlook. The Gladstonian party was Peelite in its general approach, with its practical objectives of efficiency, sound administration, limited reform, free trade and a careful approach to government expenditure.

d) A Supremely Useful Statesman?

By the late 1850s the world of Peel was only a memory, but he was the man who had worked to fashion a compromise between the system he inherited and the necessities of the new industrial society, and who had helped to efface the old Wellingtonian image of a class resolutely opposed to reform. In that sense, he forms an essential link between the world of the early-nineteenth century and the later period. In the shifting and changing times in which he lived, he was well-suited to guide the Conservative Party and the country into a more peaceful era of contentment and stability. As one of Disraeli's own characters wrote in *Coningsby*, 'What is the use of lamenting the past. Peel is the man; suited to the times and all that; at least we must say so and try to believe so; we can't go back'.

Making notes on '*Conservatism, 1832-46: The Age of Peel*'

Your notes need to cover certain key areas of Peel's work, both in office and in opposition. (You will already have recorded information on his work at the Home Office in the 1820s.) On the period to 1841, notes can be brief, and could use these headings;

> The state of the Tory Party after 1832
> The policy directions open to Peel
> First Ministry (1834-5)
> The Tamworth Manifesto
> Electoral progress to 1841
> Organisational reform

You should ensure that you have a clear idea of the ways in which he restored Conservative fortunes in the 1830s, and why his performance in opposition is often considered to be highly creditable. However, most of your attention should be focused on his Second Ministry of 1841-6, and you should cover;

> A strong Cabinet
> Financial policies; taxation, duties, Companies and Banking Acts
> Social changes
> Ireland
> The Corn laws; why he repealed them, why the issue caused controversy, opposition to repeal in and out of his party, the fate of Peel and his government

For each of the policies he introduced, be sure that you are clear why he thought they were necessary; eg, what was the problem in the national finances which he sought to remedy? Then see whether you think that the outcome of his changes made things significantly better.

At this stage, it will be worth constructing a paragraph identifying the issues to be considered when assessing Peel's significance in the history of his party.

Opposition 1832-41	Office 1841-6
1832 Peel becomes Leader in House of Commons	1841 Peel PM
1834-5 PM Tamworth Manifesto	Financial Policy
	- Free Trade
	- Income Tax
	- Ending Whig deficit
	- Commercial legislation
	- Mines Act
	- Factory Act
1835-41 Opposition	
- New Conservatism	
- Responsible Opposition	Social Policy
- Electoral Improvement 1835 and 1837	
1841 Victory in general election	1846 Repeal of Corn Laws
	Tory split into Protectionists and Peelites

Summary - Conservatism, 1832-46: The Age of Peel

Answering essay questions on *'Conservatism, 1832-46: The Age of Peel'*

Essays tend to be set on two aspects of Peel's contribution. Some are based on his 'great reforming ministry'. A typical example is:

1 To what extent did the domestic policies of Peel's Second Ministry indicate that he possessed a sympathetic appreciation of the needs of an industrial society?

His financial and social policies need to be reviewed, but a key element in your answer will concern his attitude to the Corn Laws, the repeal of which he thought was very important in easing the burdens on the labouring classes in England and Ireland. You need to ask yourself what the 'needs of an industrial society' were; these would include moves to promote the development of industry and commerce, but also to provide social and political stability, by making the nation more at ease with itself. If Peel did possess this 'sympathetic appreciation', from where did he gain this insight? Was it his background? 'To what extent?' again features in the phraseology of the question; ask yourself how far Peel's approach to the relative importance of agriculture and industry suggested such an appreciation. If he understood the need to promote the interests of industry and commerce, did he also appreciate that in an industrialising society there would be a need for measures to protect the workers?

Other questions relate more directly to his personal qualities and contribution. An example of this type of question is:

2   Discuss the view that Peel's unrivalled record of achievement made him the pre-eminent British statesman of his time.

Consider his achievements, remembering to look back to his work in the 1820s as Home Secretary, including his approach to the Catholic question. Refer to his attitude to parliamentary reform in 1830-2, as well as his work in the 1830s and 1840s. Think about the words 'unrivalled' and 'pre-eminent'; questions usually have key words in them, and you need to consider their implications. In this case, it would be helpful if you knew something of the other leading figures of the period. Also, you might consider whether his 'achievement' was for the benefit of his party or of his country.

This aspect features in another type of question, in which you are asked to:

3   Discuss the view that 'Peel was too ready to sacrifice the interests of his party to what he believed were those of the country'.

Here, you obviously need to consider the interests of the party and those of the nation. Strong party supporters wish to see their party stick to its traditional attitudes, and feel uncomfortable with a departure from them. Yet they also wish to see the party win elections. The interests of the nation may seem to necessitate the pursuit of policies which could be contrary to party principle; however, if pursuing them makes the country more prosperous and the people more contented, might this not benefit the party's prospects at the polls? Or was this less true when most people were still unable to vote anyway? Was Peel, as Disraeli claimed, too willing to abandon his party's principles, too prone to the political 'U-turn'? Consider especially his behaviour over Catholic Emancipation, Maynooth and the Corn Laws.

Think about some of these issues, and then construct a diagrammatic plan (of the type shown on page 47) to prepare an answer to question 3.

Source-based questions on 'Conservatism, 1832-46: The Age of Peel'

1 The Tamworth Manifesto, 1835

Carefully read the extract from the Tamworth Manifesto on page 54. Answer the following questions.

a) What did Peel mean by an acceptance of the 'spirit' of the 1832 Reform Bill? (5 marks)
b) What do the language and tone of the extract convey about the nature of Peel as a Conservative reformer? (5 marks)
c) What are the strengths and weaknesses of the Tamworth Manifesto as a guide to Conservative Party thinking in the 1830s? (6 marks)
d) On the evidence of this extract, how much truth was there in Disraeli's claim that 'The Tamworth Manifesto was an attempt to construct a party without principles' and that its inevitable consequence was 'Political Infidelity'? (4 marks)

2 Peel and the Repeal of the Corn Laws

Carefully read the three extracts on pages 63 and 66. Answer the following questions.

a) What did Goulburn believe to be the possible consequences if Peel changed his mind over the Corn Laws? (2 marks)
b) To what extent did Disraeli's attack bear out Goulburn's fears? (3 marks)
c) How reliable are Disraeli's comments as a guide to the standing of Peel in the Conservative Party in 1845-6? (3 marks)
d) What priority would the three speakers have given to a) party, and b) country, in deciding what should have been done by Peel about the Corn Law question? (6 marks)
e) It was said of Peel over the issue of the Maynooth Grant, that 'he changeth with the time'. How far would the three speakers have agreed with such a viewpoint? (6 marks)

3 Peel and the Young Disraeli

Study the cartoon on page 64, and the relations between them as described on pages 57 and 65-8. Answer the following questions.

a) What was Disraeli's initial reaction to Peel's leadership? (4 marks)
b) For what reasons before the issue of the Repeal of the Corn Laws had Disraeli come to dislike the leadership of Peel? (6 marks)
c) In what ways in 1845-6 did the young Disraeli set out to 'smash' Peel's leadership? (5 marks)
d) Which of them emerged with a more enhanced reputation after the events of that session? (5 marks)

CHAPTER 5

From Peel to Disraeli, 1846-81

1 Introduction

The Repeal of the Corn Laws ushered in a period of confusion and instability in British politics. During the first part of Peel's great ministry there had seemed to be something akin to a two-party system in operation, but in 1845-6 this had no longer been the case, and Peel had needed Whig support to carry through repeal. After the break-up of the Conservatives, party ties continued, but the labels did not mean very much, and the personalities of key individuals - Peel himself, Disraeli, Gladstone and Palmerston - assumed more significance. Over the next 20 years or so the fortunes of these men largely determined the fate of governments, which could never be sure of securing a majority. This was because there were no strong parties, and the discipline of Conservative voting which characterised the period 1835-45 had largely disappeared.

In these years there were few major issues which divided opinion in parliament. Occasionally public feeling might be aroused, as over the conduct of the Crimean War, but for much of the time politics was less than lively. This was partly because by the 1850s the country was becoming more prosperous, with most classes benefiting to some degree from better living standards. Improved conditions made for an easing of social tensions, and even a subject such as parliamentary reform ceased to stir the popular imagination. Many people seemed to be willing to leave such matters to their political masters, so that in his *The English Constitution* Walter Bagehot could write, 'The English Constitution in its palpable form is this - the mass of the people yield obedience to a select few'.

It was to be the successful passage of the 1867 Reform Bill by the minority Conservative government which changed the political landscape and introduced a new style of electioneering and political organisation into British life. Having been for so long in the wilderness, the Conservatives needed some bold stroke to re-establish themselves as a credible political force. It was Disraeli who provided it, for his Bill was a daring manoeuvre which outflanked the efforts of the Liberals (as the former Whig party was now popularly called) in its bold radicalism. In the short term the move did him little good, for the Conservatives lost the 1868 election which followed the passing of the Second Reform Act. In the longer term the gamble paid handsome dividends. It had shown that the party was capable of governing, and in the general election of 1874 Disraeli was rewarded with a parliamentary majority which ensured him a worthwhile spell in office (1874-80). It is on the basis of his performance during his time as Prime Minister that much of Disraeli's reputation rests.

2 Personalities and Policies

The issue which did much to bring about the state of party confusion and which had such a disastrous impact upon Conservative fortunes was, of course, protection. The Party was effectively out of power for a generation, despite the fact that Conservative governments took office on three occasions under the leadership of Lord Derby - in 1852, 1858-9 and 1866-8. On each occasion they were in a minority position, and the years 1846-65 were ones when Whig-Liberal politicians were in the ascendancy.

Peel's apostasy over the Corn Laws had created a situation in which there were two groups of Conservatives at Westminster - the Protectionists and the Peelites. Peel had decided that Repeal was the duty of the government but he had done little to prepare the party to support a measure which he had previously opposed. Repeal offended his party's natural inclinations as well as threatening to damage the pockets of many of its supporters. Peel had expected them to follow him but many Conservatives shared Disraeli's view that parties stood for certain broad principles and policies, and that the ones to which the Conservatives laid a special claim were the Church and the landed interest.

a) The Peelites

As long as Sir Robert Peel lived he was the undisputed leader of those who had supported him in 1846. He never resigned the leadership, but he was unwilling to give any sort of lead. Neither did he make any attempt to reunite the party whose fortunes he had done so much to restore. Both before and immediately after his death in 1850 the Peelites gave broad support to the Whig government of Lord John Russell. They called themselves Conservatives but they shared with the Whigs a commitment to free trade.

Peel's influence lived on for many years via the group of influential supporters with which he had surrounded himself. Chief among these was his arch-disciple, Gladstone, who had been puzzled and disappointed by Peel's stance after 1846. He could not understand how his old leader could let the Conservative Party collapse, and in effect say 'it has fallen, there let it lie'. However, he and others remained faithful to their dead leader's memory, especially in their devotion to free trade and financial economy. They were in a difficult position and it was tempting to revert to old allegiances. After all, they were Conservatives by choice and by tradition, and had a deep attachment to the party. Some did hanker after a reunion with their former comrades, but most could not bring themselves to contemplate it. They deeply distrusted Disraeli, none more so than Gladstone, who could never forgive the cruel vindictiveness of his earlier attacks on Peel.

Yet neither did the Whigs appear to be an attractive alternative. In particular, Palmerston, the Foreign Secretary, had little appeal for them. They felt that his forceful and bombastic foreign policy was wrong in both principle and practice. In domestic affairs he was perhaps less willing to contemplate change and improvement than Disraeli. He did, however, have the advantage of possessing considerable support in the country, and of the two evils, he was perhaps the lesser. He and the Whigs also had support from the Radicals, among whom were Cobden and Bright with whom the Peelites were substantially agreed on free trade and foreign policy.

For some time, the Peelites (or Liberal Conservatives as some called themselves) remained a separate group, declining in power and influence as time passed. Having 'no organisation, no whipper-in', they were, in Gladstone's words, 'a public nuisance'. They had a foot in both parties but they belonged to neither. Gradually, however, the more prominent among them joined with the Liberal Party and came to invigorate it with their beliefs and with their intellectual prowess.

b) The Protectionists

After the break-up in 1846 the Protectionist group largely consisted of back-bench country gentlemen, with Bentinck and Disraeli there to rally them. Most of the brains and much of the talent of the Conservative Party had sided with Peel, which lends substance to the appellation which the Radical, John Stuart Mill, used when he called the Conservatives the 'stupid party'. Whatever their intellectual shortcomings, they were the country party defending the interests of agriculture, which were also their own interests.

The Protectionists had a solid corps of support at Westminster but this did not provide the foundations for a wider party of popular feeling, for outside the ranks of the farming community no one wanted protection. It had not been difficult for Disraeli to exploit the self-interest of the gentry and rally them for a fight against repeal. It was harder to get the party back upon its feet again, the more so as even Disraeli recognised that protection had run its useful course, and was no longer a politically viable policy.

However, in seeking to shed the commitment to protection, Disraeli was asking his supporters to go against those instincts which he had encouraged them to express. The attempt inevitably aroused suspicions about his character and motives, for some members of the landed class felt that they had been used to further Disraeli's own career interests. Nevertheless, despite the risks, by 1852 he was saying to an old friend that protection was 'not only dead, but damned'. He hoped that his renunciation would help to win Gladstone, Graham, Cardwell and others back into the Conservative fold, but, like some of his own supporters, they were unconvinced about his sincerity and could not trust him.

c) Conservative Policies and Progress

After 1846 Protectionists and Peelites sat on the same Front Bench, Disraeli only three seats away from Peel. However, the future of the Conservative cause now lay with the Protectionists, led at first by Bentinck and Disraeli. Their leadership was soon faced with an embarrassment when a practising Jew was elected for the City of London. Jews were not allowed in the House of Commons but both men believed that they should be. Disraeli flung himself into the battle for Jewish admission when a bill was presented to parliament, arguing that Jews should be admitted as equals in a Christian country 'because they can show so near an affinity to you. Where is your Christianity if you do not let in their Judaism?'

Many of the squires on the Conservative back benches were less than convinced. For them Jewish birth and Tory politics were not easy bedfellows. The stand taken by Bentinck and Disraeli was generally unsupported in the party, and there was much criticism from the rank and file. This led to Bentinck's resignation, and opened up the question of the succession. Disraeli had obvious flair, but at this stage did not have much experience and there were doubts about his trustworthiness. But there was no one else who was nearly as effective as a parliamentary performer, There were few able rivals: most were too old, too inexperienced or too lacking in basic competence. Therefore, almost by default, Disraeli became leader of the Conservative Party in the House of Commons in January 1849. Lord Stanley led the party in the Lords and was its senior figure.

d) Lord Derby (Lord Stanley until 1851)

When Lord Stanley was offered the leadership of the Protectionists he faced a daunting task, for many of the ablest politicians were in the Peelite ranks. Few of the country squires were capable or valued spokesman. Indeed, many had rarely spoken before the Corn Law controversy - not for nothing did Bagehot see the Tory gentry as 'the finest brute-vote in creation'. Few backbenchers were of cabinet potential and there were even doubts about Stanley's qualifications. Many Conservatives commented on his 'cynical insincerity' and found him to be a none-too-scrupulous grandee. He was lighthearted and did not take his task too seriously, being more interested in horses. He was at home on the turf, and was a steward of the Jockey Club. This distracted his attention, and Disraeli found his approach to leadership frustrating, complaining that, 'There are a thousand things which ought to be done ... and which I am obliged to decline doing or to do at great sacrifice. As for our Chief, we never see him'. Derby enjoyed his life, never wished to be a full-time politician, and was in his own words, 'devoted to whist, billiards, racing, [and] betting'.

He contributed little to the intellectual development of Conservatism, for he was no party philosopher. Above all he was content to coast along. As his son told Disraeli, 'the Captain does not care for office, but wishes to keep things as they are and impede "progress"'.

e) Derby's Ministries

Disraeli was hungry for office and this required a strengthened Conservative Party. Hence the effort to bury Protectionism and to entice the Peelites back into the fold. For a while he was frustrated because in 1851 his leader failed to form a government because he did not have enough talent available. Stanley knew he was scraping the bottom of the barrel, and exclaimed 'Pshaw! These are not names I can put before the queen'. Disraeli was both furious and depressed, for the cup of office had been dashed from his lips, and it was this experience which made him realise that Protection must be 'unequivocally removed'.

In 1852 the chance came again, and this time Lord Derby formed his first government. Lord Palmerston, a Whig, was offered the Exchequer, but declined to serve, and few other parliamentarians of any note did agree. The Duke of Wellington was not even approached; now an old man, and hard of hearing, he repeatedly inquired 'Who, who?' when the Cabinet names were read to him, and in so doing provided a label for the ministry which was named after his question. Most of the ministers were inexperienced, and when Disraeli admitted he had 'no knowledge of the subject-matter of his position' (as Chancellor), he was reassured by the Prime Minister that this did not matter, for 'They give you the figures'. Disraeli produced his Budget proposals, but they were defeated in the House of Commons in December 1852, and Derby immediately resigned.

In 1858 Derby again became Prime Minister at the head of a minority government. This time some of the dead wood in the last ministry had been removed and there were some new and more able recruits. Disraeli, again the Chancellor, was very keen to see a revival of Conservative fortunes and was searching for a strategy which might bring about success. He tried to persuade Derby to seize the initiative on an extension of the franchise, pointing out that; 'Our party is now a corpse, but it appears to me that, in the present perplexed state of affairs, a Conservative public pledge to parliamentary reform, a bold and decided course, might not only put us on our legs, but greatly help the country'. However, the practical difficulties of producing an agreed scheme were enormous and the bill which Disraeli drew up was insufficiently appealing to gain necessary parliamentary support from the Opposition. The government was defeated in a Commons vote and went out of office after the subsequent election.

Nonetheless, although he failed on this occasion to keep the Conservatives in power, by 1860 Disraeli felt able to take credit for his achievement in 'educating his party' and making it look ready for government. He claimed:

1 I found the Tory Party in the House of Commons, when I acceded
   to its chief management, in a state of great depression and
   disorganisation ... I withdrew the ... party gradually from the
   hopeless question of protection, rallied all those members who
5 were connected either personally or by their constituencies with
   the land, and finally brought the state of parties in the House of
   Commons nearly to a tie.

Seven years later Derby was back again in Downing Street to lead another minority government with Disraeli as leader in the House of Commons. This time the events leading up to the formation of the ministry were very different. Palmerston, whose opposition had acted as a brake upon reform, was dead, and Gladstone had taken up the cause of parliamentary reform. With Russell, the Prime Minister, also in favour, Gladstone had put forward the government's proposals but they had been seen as too mild for most Radicals and too radical for most Whigs. The government was defeated in the House of Commons in 1866 by a combination of dissident Whig-Liberals and Conservatives. Russell resigned and the Conservatives returned.

f) Parliamentary Reform, 1867

It was important for the Conservatives to show that this time they could stay in power sufficiently long to establish that they were a party of government. If they could rally their own supporters and by their proposals divide the Liberals, then there was a chance that this might happen. The time was ripe for another attempt at enacting a measure of parliamentary reform.

Disraeli seized the initiative with a bold stroke of political opportunism. He was a master of the political arts and welcomed his chance to produce a measure which would identify the Conservatives as a party of reform and ensure the ministry's survival. He needed to act quickly because he wished to exploit existing Liberal disagreements over the franchise question in order to establish his own ascendancy in the party. Lord Derby's health was failing and if Disraeli could come up with a political success it might stand him in good stead when the leadership of the Conservatives became vacant.

The actual passage of the bill and Disraeli's twists and turns do not matter here, although they do illustrate his parliamentary skills. Suffice it to say that his performance was widely recognised as a *tour de force,* for he manoeuvred adroitly to attract backing from any possible section of the House, even accepting amendments whose implications he did not fully comprehend.

By the time the Derby-Disraeli proposals had been discussed in the House of Commons they were far more radical than had been intended. Some sections had been lifted directly from Gladstone's Bill, while others had been taken on board along the way. Above all, the Conservatives had put an act on the statute book, and its effects on British political life were to be enormous. Although the redistribution of seats from the less populous to the industrial areas was modest, and nothing was done to tackle corruption, the right to vote was extended considerably. In the counties the electorate went up by nearly 50 per cent but it was in the industrial boroughs where the changes were more sweeping, and where the effects were to be so dramatic. The skilled manual workers were to be enfranchised, for the measure gave the vote to all householders who paid rates and lodgers who paid £10 a year in rent. In Leeds, for example, the number of electors rose from 8,500 to 35,000.

Even Derby described the measure as a 'leap in the dark' and a 'giant experiment'. Some suspected that Disraeli had deceived them and for others there was great anxiety. To Lord Carnarvon, personally a critic, the result constituted 'a revolution. The Conservative Party is in imminent danger of going to pieces now, if indeed it does not disappear in the deluge that the government are bringing on'. Like Cranborne, the future Lord Salisbury, who also feared the growth of democracy, he resigned from the government.

Disraeli had privately indicated to Bright that 'the working class question was the real question', and that was the thing that demanded to be settled in a far more radical way than Disraeli originally intended. As a result of his actions, the whole balance of power in British politics had been shifted. For the result was that the working classes constituted a majority of voters in the boroughs, which in turn now made up a majority of the constituencies.

Disraeli had said of Peel that 'he caught the Whigs out bathing and made off with their clothes'. His backbenchers thought that he had now done the same, and whilst many admired his tactical skill others felt bamboozled and deceived. However, the Act was artfully designed to minimise the novel situation of an enlarged electorate. The fact that the franchise in the towns was tied to a property qualification, that many small boroughs had been placed within Conservative county seats and that the South and West remained so over-represented made sceptics realise that all was not lost, and that there was some hope of 'taming the new democracy'.

The clash in 1867 was one of the first major parliamentary battles between Gladstone and Disraeli who were to be such formidable adversaries in the years ahead. Gladstone concentrated on the precise details, and attempted to expose the Bill's inadequacies. Disraeli managed to isolate him and to establish a temporary Tory-Radical alliance. For the moment Disraeli seemed to have the advantage. Derby had not been well for some time, and in February 1868 he resigned. On his advice the queen sent for Disraeli as the new Prime Minister. At a party thrown in his honour he agreed that 'Yes, I have climbed to the top of the greasy pole'. Bright, who had watched his performance in the House over several years, observed that this was 'a great triumph of intelligence and patience', the more remarkable in a 'party full of prejudices and wanting in brains'.

g) Disraeli, His Background and Early Career

Benjamin Disraeli was born in 1804 the grandson of a Jewish immigrant who had changed the family name from D'Israeli into its more acceptable form. His father had sent the young boy to local private schools and had had him baptised into the Christian faith, as an Anglican. The young Benjamin began his working career as a writer. His first novel, *Vivian Grey*, was published in 1826. His hero was, in his own words, 'an elegant lively lad with just enough of dandyism to preserve him from committing gaucheries, and with the devil of a tongue'. The description is not unlike Disraeli himself.

It was not easy to take the young Disraeli seriously for he was reckless in his personal life. He was a gambler - constantly in debt - who led a 'raffish' life-style and had several relationships with married women. He remarked that 'my nature demands that my life should be perpetual love', and he did much to ensure that this requirement was met. But when he met Mrs Wyndham Lewis, 12 years his senior, his life was changed. In 1837 she persuaded her husband to allow Disraeli the use of the family rotten borough of Maidstone as a way of entering the House of Commons, and when she became widowed two years later the two of them married. Marriage provided Disraeli with enough money to clear his accumulated debts. In addition, his new wife gave him support and took his aspirations seriously; 'she believed in me, when men despised me'.

In the 1830s he had made five unsuccessful attempts to enter the House of Commons, firstly as a Radical, then as an Independent, and finally as a Conservative. Maidstone was the solution to his difficulties and he joined the ranks of the backbenchers who supported Sir Robert Peel. The Maiden Speech which he made was a fiasco. As always he was extravagantly dressed - bedecked with bangles and jewels, and reeking of exotic perfume. It was not surprising that MPs did not take his remarks seriously. Although his speech was carefully prepared, its numerous classical allusions and convoluted style were not well attuned to the audience, so that by the end he was being hooted down in derision. This provoked his famous reply, 'I sit down now, but the time will come when you will hear me!'.

Fortunately, he was well advised by an Irish MP to 'get rid of your genius' for a while, 'Speak often ... be very quiet, try to be dull ...

astonish them by speaking on subjects of detail. Quote figures, dates, calculations, and in a short time the House will sigh for the wit and eloquence which they all know are in you'. Less ostentatious dress and demeanour helped him along too, and soon he did acquire a reputation as a lively speaker and a spirited debater.

At first he was a loyal supporter of Peel - 'the only hope of England' - and, although he was disillusioned by his failure to gain office in 1841, he generally voted for Peelite measures until 1843. Then he began to develop a distrust for the Prime Minister's approach, seeing him as insufficiently strong in his convictions. At first, he criticised his Conservatism rather than the man himself, and denounced 'Tory men and Whig measures'. But then the attack was widened. He teamed up with some young aristocrats who had entered the House in 1841 and they collectively referred to themselves as the 'Young England' group. George Smythe and Lord John Manners were leading members. They and others became the basis for characters in *Coningsby*, Disraeli's novel which was published in 1844, and in which the Tamworth Manifesto was attacked as an 'attempt to construct a party without principles'. They all shared a similar desire to return to earlier days before the dawn of industrialisation, times when landed Tories ruled the nation. In the words of Manners,

> Let wealth and commerce, laws and learning die
> But leave us still our old nobility.

Young England members came to despise the consensus politics of the Peelite party, so influenced by the new forces of industry and commerce. They hankered for a return to the days when the aristocracy possessed a paternalistic role as defenders of the mass of people from the evils of industrial life. They strongly disliked the New Poor Law of 1834, with its hated 'bastilles', and showed some sympathy for the Chartists, whilst not approving of any extreme behaviour. They were, in Blake's words, 'Swimming against the tide, but it was not an ignoble effort to want to see a return to a less harsh world'.

The group faded away after its members divided over the right approach to adopt over the Maynooth Grant (see pages 61-2), and they were similarly divided over the Repeal of the Corn Laws. On both issues Disraeli was on the opposite side to Peel, representing the Ultras rather than the new Conservatism which was so much more appealing to middle-class men of business. By his oratory and, in particular, the scathing attacks on Peel and his creed, he was damaging not only the Prime Minister but also the party. If Peel might have handled the Corn Laws with more tactical skill and concern for people's feelings, it was nonetheless Disraeli who so effectively 'put the boot in' and by his actions helped to put the party out of office for a generation.

After the splitting up of the Conservative Party Disraeli controlled the fortunes of the anti-Peelite forces, even if the formal leadership lay in the hands of Bentinck and Stanley. They had the titles and connections, and were more obvious leaders of a primarily landed party. But Disraeli had the flair which was so much needed, and well before he reached the top, his ability was widely conceded. *The Times* commented on his contribution in 1860.

1 Let the Conservative Party never forget the hopeless state in which they were when fortune sent them Mr Disraeli for a leader. They had grown weary of a chief who was too liberal for their views of national policy, and avenged themselves upon him by an act of
5 renunciation which left them without leaders. They were irretrievably committed to an unpopular cause. Gradually, Mr Disraeli has weaned his party from their most flagrant errors. He has taught them to profess a sympathy for the great body of their countrymen and to recognise the necessity of looking to public
10 opinion for support. When he found the Tory Party, they were armed in impenetrable prejudice; under him, they have become competitors with the Liberals in the career of progress.

Not so much in the pursuit of this 'progress', but more with the aim of making his party credible and fit for a prolonged spell in office, he 'dished the Whigs' in 1867 over parliamentary reform. After this he was the obvious contender for the vacant leadership when Derby retired from the scene. Until then he was by his own description 'the educator of his party', the man who had done so much to wean it from old attitudes and make it come to terms with the current situation.

h) How and why Disraeli got to the Top

Disraeli's rise 'to the top of the greasy pole' was a remarkable and in some ways surprising achievement. He possessed many seeming disadvantages which he was fond of recalling in later life. Victorian England was a status-ridden society, and governments were garrisoned by gentlemen of great wealth. He appeared to lack most of the obvious qualifications for leadership of a party which numbered so many titled names amongst its members.

As he portrayed his past, he had been a nobody, he came from a poor background, and had attended no famous school or university. Moreover, he was a Jew, and every habit and tradition of the age made this seem an insuperable barrier to surmount. He had been compelled 'to struggle against a storm of political hate and malice which few men ever experienced'. Of course, to some extent this was a result of his own wounding speeches and the distrust which his behaviour inspired.

These disadvantages have often been exaggerated. His father was comfortably off and marriage eased his financial problems and helped to put his 'doubtful' early reputation behind him. He certainly lacked rank but he was able to buy himself into the landowning fraternity by purchasing a manor house at Hughenden in 1848. This gave him property, even though he never lived the usual life of a country gentleman, and he neither shot nor hunted. Similarly, baptism into Christianity gave him religious respectability. However, his Jewishness was still a barrier at a time when anti-semitism was rife. At the end of his disastrous maiden speech in the House of Commons, there had been derisive references to 'Shylock', which was how *Punch* portrayed him. Lord Cranborne, later to be his successor at the helm, dismissed him as a 'Jewish adventurer'.

Even allowing for the fact that the barriers he had to overcome were exaggerated, it was no mean achievement for Disraeli to reach the top, because there is no doubt that he arrived there against the wishes and despite the prejudices of many in his party. That he did so was partly a matter of ability. He was a superb parliamentarian - skilful and courageous, and a master of the inimitable turn of phrase. He was often opposed by many great performers in the House of Commons, but he invariably countered their oratory with resourcefulness, ingenuity and his own particular eloquence. His speaking and debating talent was recognised by Derby, who acknowledged the ability even if he doubted the honour of his colleague. Lord Malmesbury, a future Foreign Secretary, also observed it and on Bentinck's resignation he remarked that, 'no-one but Disraeli can fill his place ... it will leave [him] without a rival, and enable him to show the great genius he undoubtedly possesses'.

The observation points to another key fact - the absence of any real competition. Bentinck had remarked that Disraeli was 'the only man who came up to his ideas as an orator'. The longer the party had remained in the wilderness, the more it was apparent that there was no one else of remotely comparable quality. He was still not liked by many Conservatives and was seen as an outsider but, despite his lack of rank and alien race, he established an obvious ascendancy over those around him.

i) Disraeli's Character

Disraeli was one of the most colourful personalities of the nineteenth century. He had abundant charm, and women found him particularly attractive. His conversation was witty and sparkling, and he was a romantic, with a past reputation as a *roué*. The hint of disrepute made him all the more interesting, and his pleasing manner, with its lack of pomposity, was enough to beguile many. He was also an arch-flatterer who told women, in particular, what they were pleased to hear. The queen was susceptible to his engaging personality and appreciated his flattery, and he saw that, when dealing with royalty, it should be laid on

Disraeli, 1869: by 'Ape', Vanity Fair

'with a trowel'. He adored female company and was more at ease within
it. Surrounded by men he could feel lonely and awkward.

His wife doted on him and he was devoted to her. It was a marriage
which remained fresh and young, and he told her that she was 'more of a
mistress to him than a wife'. From his early days his easy relationship
with women gave him an *entrée* into the fringes of London society, and
once he had a foot in the door he was able to impress people with his
charm and wit. He had a great desire to make a name for himself and win
renown so that he could make a lasting impression in his chosen career
as a writer and politician.

Whereas in his younger days he was often described as 'adventurous'
and 'imaginative', among the more flattering epithets, by his twilight
times he had so gained in popular appeal that he acquired a new dignity
and air of authority. His earlier rakishness and disreputableness had
been absorbed into a different image in which he was still exotic but was
also a figure of drama, romance and mystery. His death left Westminster
a duller place for by then parliament had come to respect him. Until his
last days, when his concentration and energy were undermined by ill
health, his performance always commanded attention..

j) Disraeli as Prime Minister, 1868, and in Opposition, 1868-74

Disraeli's ministry was a short one for his government was still in a
parliamentary minority. He called for a dissolution as soon as the new
electoral registers were ready. The new electorate did not reward him,
for as JS Mill remarked, it said 'Thank you, Mr Gladstone'. The
Conservatives were soundly beaten and Gladstone become Prime
Minister.

Out of office Disraeli soon successfully resumed his career as a
novelist. Generally he was content to sit back and allow his arch enemy
to make mistakes, and there was some dissatisfaction within the Party at
his lack of positive leadership. Attempts were made to replace him with
the Earl of Derby, son of the old Prime Minister, but he withstood the
challenge and his political fortunes began to improve as the Liberals ran
into difficulties.

Disraeli had deliberately opted for low-key opposition while he took
steps to put the party organisation into better shape. However, by 1872
he felt ready to launch his offensive against the government. In a speech
given at Manchester, for which he fortified himself with two bottles of
brandy which he slipped into his water-jug, he mocked the Liberal Front
Bench;

1 As I sat opposite the Treasury bench, the Ministers reminded me
  of one of those marine landscapes not very unusual on the coasts of
  South America. You behold a range of exhausted volcanoes. Not a
  flame flickers on a single pallid crest. But the situation is still

5 dangerous. There are occasional earthquakes, and ever and anon
the dark rumbling of the sea.

He also pointed to Gladstone's preoccupation with political reform, at
the expense of social improvement, and stressed that 'the first
consideration of a minister should be the health of the people'. He
coined the phrase *'sanitas sanitatum, onmia sanitas'*, a parody of a
Biblical allusion, which loses something in translation - 'health of health,
all is health'. He condemned the Liberals for their irreverent attitude to
established institutions, and stressed Conservative loyalty to the
monarchy, the House of Lords and the Church of England. He also
denounced the government's supine attitude in foreign policy, and
spoke of Britain's might and imperial destiny.

However, it was in his speech at the Crystal Palace later in 1872 that
he developed his themes, although he spoke firstly of the state of the
party over the past generation:

1 A long period of power and prosperity had induced it to sink into a
  state of apathy and indifference ... the Tory system had
  degenerated into a policy which found an adequate basis on the
  principles of exclusiveness and restriction. Gentleman, the Tory
5 Party unless it is a national party is nothing. It is not a confederacy
  of nobles, it is not a democratic multitude; it is a party formed from
  all the numerous classes in the realm ... Now, I have always been of
  the opinion that the Tory Party has three great objects. The first is
  to maintain the institutions of the country ... Gentlemen, there is
10 another ... object of the Tory Party - to uphold the Empire of
  England ... Another great object of the Tory Party is the elevation
  of the condition of the people.
    The health of the people [is] the most important question for a
  statesman. It involves the state of the dwellings of the people, the
15 moral consequences of which are not less considerable than the
  physical. It involves their enjoyment of some of the chief elements
  of nature - air, light and water. It involves the regulation of their
  industry, the inspection of their toil. It involves that purity of their
  provisions ... A leading member of the Liberal party described this
20 ... as 'the policy of sewage'. Well, it may be the 'policy of sewage' to
  a Liberal Member of Parliament. But to one of the labouring
  population ... it is not a 'policy of sewage', but a question of life and
  death ...

There was not much detail in his remarks, but their tone was
inspirational, and they amounted to a shrewd bid by Disraeli for
working-class support. Moreover, from 1872 the Liberals had appeared
to lose their grip and the pendulum seemed to be swinging the
Conservatives' way. The government had legislated impressively but by
now divisions were apparent. Some Liberals wanted more radical

reform while the Whigs were troubled by Gladstone's desire for change. When Gladstone contemplated resignation in the hope that Disraeli and the Conservatives would take over, Disraeli was too wily to be trapped in this way. He wanted to see the government fall, but not until it had made itself even more unpopular and suffered further setbacks in by-elections.

Eventually, a general election was called in 1874 and Gladstone's government was soundly beaten. It had trampled on too many vested interests and had offended too many groups. In particular, a substantial section of the wealthier middle classes switched their allegiance to Disraeli, whose promise of a more active foreign and imperial policy, and a rest from harassing legislation, appealed to them. An article in the *Fortnightly Review* by a contemporary Radical lamented that,

1 The real truth is that the middle class has swung round to Conservatism, of a vague and negative kind, for 'leaving well alone'. When we look at the poll in all the centres of middle-class industry, wealth and cultivation, we see that the rich trading class,
5 and the comfortable middle class has grown distinctly Conservative.

Disraeli had given the party a more attractive image and had preached a new set of Tory ideals. He thought of them as being Tory because he disliked the use of the word 'Conservative' which seemed all too reminiscent of the policies of the 1830s and 1840s. Furthermore, he had appreciated that in a more democratic age elections could be decided by party organisation, and enough had been done to put the Tories into fighting shape (see pages 105-6). The party was now fit for government in a way that it had not been since the age of Peel. There were several able men in charge, armed with an improved organisation and a new policy. They formed the first majority Conservative government since 1841.

k) Disraeli's Second Ministry, 1874-80

Disraeli was back in office for what was to be his last administration. In some ways his best years were past. As he later remarked, 'Ah, Power! It has come too late. There were days when, on waking, I felt I could move dynasties and governments; but that has passed away'. Now, he was beset by kidney disease, asthma and gout. Yet despite his advancing years and physical decline, he was not out of touch with the needs of the time. He formed a strong government and, unlike Gladstone, he had a gift for gathering able young men around him. The Cabinet contained several new and talented ministers. Lord Salisbury (formerly Lord Cranborne) had been persuaded to serve, and Richard Cross became an energetic Home Secretary.

Power had come but how would Disraeli use it? He had 'educated his party' and laid down general principles. He specialised in the broad sweep, but he could be tantalisingly vague on specifics. Ministers were left to fill in the details, and were alarmed to find that almost nothing was prepared by way of legislation.

l) Disraeli and Social Reform: His Early Outlook and Record

In his novels and in many of his speeches Disraeli had drawn attention to the shocking conditions in which millions of people lived. He had demanded that the government take firm action to put an end to these evils, and at the 1841 election, felt able to claim that 'There is no subject in which I have taken a deeper interest than the condition of the working class'.

The views expressed in those novels concerned the gulf between rich and poor. His publication of *Sybil; or the Two Nations* (1845), indicated his early approach, for in it he contrasted the two social classes which existed in England. On the one hand, there were riches and luxury, on the other, poverty and misery;

1 'Well, society may be in its infancy,' said Egremont, slightly smiling, 'but, say what you like, our Queen reigns over the greatest nation that ever existed.'
   'Which nation?', asked the stranger, 'for she reigns over two'.
5 The stranger paused; Egremont was silent, but looked inquiringly.
   'Yes,' resumed the younger stranger after a moment's interval.
   'Two nations; between whom there is no intercourse and no sympathy; who are as ignorant of each other's habits, thoughts and feelings, as if they were dwellers in different zones, or inhabitants of
10 different planets; who are formed by a different breeding, and are fed by a different food, are ordered by different manners and are not governed by the same laws.'
   'You speak of - ' said Egremont, hesitatingly.
   'THE RICH AND THE POOR'.

Disraeli had an interest in social conditions, but despite his observation in 1841 it would be misleading to think that this topic was ever one of his consuming preoccupations. He was dismayed at the worst aspects of working-class conditions, but did not often concern himself with the actual details of legislation. When important issues were debated in the House of Commons, he rarely spoke up for reform, and his voting record was patchy. On the Mines Act of 1842 (see page 60) he remained silent and abstained. He voted for the Ten Hour Bill of 1844, having spoken in the debate, and supported the Health of Towns Association, a pressure group for more sanitary towns and cities. He voted against the harsh New Poor Law, but on other questions did not seem to promote improvements, and frequently abstained in the lobbies.

Later he felt that the party needed to champion social reform. He understood that the 'condition of the people' question was an important one, the more so after 1867. Reform would act as a bait for the newly-enfranchised voters. Concern for the welfare of the people would help his party at the polls, but beyond expediency, he also felt that social reform was a right and proper function for the Conservative Party and for the new generation of the aristocracy 'whose hearts are open to the responsibility of their position'. He believed in an hierarchical society, in which each class had its assigned role; the 'natural leaders of society', the gentlemen of England, would enjoy the trust of the people as long as they recognised these responsibilities. It was expedient to introduce reform, for as he put it, 'The palace is not safe, when the cottage is not happy'. But it was also a duty of the privileged orders to care for the happiness of the people.

It was a case stated in distinctly Tory terms. If its leaders acted appropriately the gulf between the 'two nations' might be reduced, and the country be more at ease with itself - though there would always be a variety of classes and interests. As Samuel Beer has written,

1 Disraeli's Government of 1874 was Tory in both senses of the word; it was a time of strong government and its policies were rationalised by distinctively Tory purposes ... In Disraeli's version of Tory Democracy, a conception of authority was joined with a 5 distinctive conception of purpose ... Each class, rank and interest would enjoy security of status.

m) Disraeli's Premiership and Social Reform

In the 1874 election Disraeli's theme was essentially negative. He had promised a 'respite from the incessant and harassing legislation' of Gladstone and the 'dangerous' Liberals. He said little about reform other than to offer a general commitment. However, the impression given was that there would be a series of improvements, for after all, in his Crystal Palace speech, he had promised measures 'to elevate the physical as well as the moral condition of the people'. At one and the same time he was a rallying point for those disturbed by excessive innovation and for those who wanted cautious, piecemeal reform. He took office, therefore, bound by no programme and committed to nothing specific. But he did have wide authority to translate some of his general ideas into particular measures.

Some of his abler colleagues in the new Cabinet were surprised to find that he had no set ideas and no detailed policies to propose. There was a lack of direction from him and the conduct of affairs was left to individuals. Richard Cross recalled the situation in his memoirs;

1 When the Cabinet came to discuss the Queen's Speech, I was, I confess, disappointed at the want of originality shown by the Prime

Minister. From all his speeches, I had quite expected that his mind
was full of legislative schemes, but such did not prove to be the
5 case; on the contrary, he had to rely on the various suggestions of
his colleagues, and as they themselves had only just come into
office, and that suddenly there, there was some difficulty in
framing the Queen's Speech.

As Sir Richard Cross, the Home Secretary, and formerly a successful
Lancashire barrister and banker, he himself deserves much of the credit
for the reforms which were achieved. He was highly competent, a good
administrator, and had a grasp of practical affairs. He represented a
progressive vein of Conservatism. Inspired by Disraeli's utterances, he
wanted to tackle the problems of people's living conditions, and he was
the author of many of the reforms which were passed. In his zeal for
innovation, Robert Blake has noted a resemblance to Neville
Chamberlain, Joseph's son, who was to prove a reforming Conservative
Health Minister under Stanley Baldwin in the 1920s.

n) The Main Reforms

Industrial towns and cities were crowded with insanitary back-to-back
dwellings, and the Artisans Dwellings Act of 1875 attempted to deal
with the problem of slum housing. Local authorities were empowered to
purchase and demolish such property, and to reconstruct whole areas.
Cross met with intense opposition from within his own party to a
measure which was seen as an infringement of the rights of private
property, and because of this he did not make the measure compulsory.
Yet, despite its permissive character, in some parts of the country the
Act was effectively employed, most notably in Birmingham. Joseph
Chamberlain, the reforming Mayor of Birmingham, had discussed the
Bill with Cross, and as a result the proposals had been improved. Using
its terms, including the availability of cheap loans, Chamberlain
produced a Birmingham Improvement Scheme which planned to clear
away the slums near the city centre. However, in the process, he
thwarted Cross's original intention that cheap working-class housing
should be built, and instead embarked on a major programme of civic
development, including the building of his new 'Boulevard', Cor-
poration Street.
    Cross also took up the cause of public health, although it had been
tackled by the Liberals. However, the legislation on the subject was still
confusing, and needed to be rationalised so that the responsibilities of
the various authorities were clearly specified. His Public Health Act
(1875) was an important and far-reaching measure, for certain statutory
duties were placed upon local councils - among other things, nuisances
were to be removed, contaminated food safely destroyed and infectious
diseases notified. Other items covered ranged from street-lighting to

burials, and it remained the basis of legislation until 1929.

In the opinion of Liberal historian, R.K. Ensor, 1875 was an *annus mirabilis* for useful domestic legislation. The Sale of Food and Drugs Act was designed to prevent the adulteration of food, and it laid down stringent regulations concerning the ways in which food was prepared. Again, this was a more comprehensive development of Gladstonian legislation, extending its terms to cover more types of food and more types of shop. Purification was also the theme of another measure. A Rivers Pollution Act attempted to limit the offensive habit of discharging poisonous liquids and solid industrial waste materials into the waterways.

As part of the attempt to improve public health and living conditions, an effort was made to provide a healthier environment. The Enclosure Act protected the public's right to use the common pasture land by stopping landlords from absorbing it into their estates. Under this legislation, Epping Forest was saved for the people of London two years later.

The Agricultural Holdings Act was piloted by Disraeli himself, and was the first of its kind in mainland Britain. It provided displaced tenants with the right to compensation for improvements carried out on their land.

On factories, the 1874 Factory Act reduced the maximum working day to 10 hours and limited the week to 56 hours, allowing for a Saturday half-day. No child could work full-time until he or she was 14. The Factory and Workshop Act (1878) distinguished between a factory and a workshop, but ensured that both types of premises should be brought under regular governmental inspection. This was an important advance in the rights accorded to industrial workers.

The labour and trade union legislation was an important breakthrough, pleasing employees and the unions. Disraeli anticipated that his new legislation would 'gain and retain for the Conservatives the lasting affection of the working classes'. The Conspiracy and Protection of Property Act of 1875 removed a grievance against Gladstone's government which had legalised trade unions but had denied them the right to engage in peaceful picketing. Cross now made picketing legal, and in a further Trade Union Act attempted to produce a clear definition of unions, and their rights and responsibilities. Old regulations against their activities were swept away.

His Employers and Workmen's Act redressed another grievance. Previously, if an employer broke a contract it was a civil wrong, which attracted only a light punishment, whilst if an employee committed the same offence, he could be charged with a breach of the criminal law. Both were put on the same footing, so that transgressions of the law were liable only to civil penalties.

By the Education Act of 1876 Lord Sandon sought to set up School Attendance Committees to ensure that children received an education.

The duty was placed on parents of making sure that their children received adequate instruction, although the government did not specify that this must be given in schools. Similarly, the Committees could help parents of needy children with the payment of school fees, but did not have to do so.

Some of the other reforms were of little consequence, but one well-known act was brought about as a result of the activity of Samuel Plimsoll. Concerned that decrepit ships were often over-loaded by unscrupulous owners, so that if the ship went down they could claim (excessively) on their insurance, he persuaded the government to introduce a Bill. Reaction among the shipowners was very strong, and they waged a campaign of obstruction before the Merchant Shipping Act reached the statute book. From then on, a maximum load-line, the 'Plimsoll line', had to be marked on every ship.

In the last years of the ministry, dogged as it was by growing trade depression, Irish obstructionism in the House of Commons, and colonial problems, the impetus to reform drained away. Disraeli became ever more immersed in matters of foreign policy, and ministers and backbenchers were pleased to have a respite from further change.

o) Assessment of the Reforms

Disraeli's own attention was largely focused elsewhere, mainly in foreign affairs. He was prepared to offer his support for Cross's actions and took a general interest in them; in particular, he was much in sympathy with the labour legislation which Cross introduced. But he was not the architect of bills himself. Indeed, of the package of measures, some might have been brought forward whichever government was in power; for instance, the Public Health Act was in the civil-service pipeline awaiting legislative action. Others such as the Pure Food and Drugs Act clarified the existing situation, and built on or modified previous laws. Few actually broke new ground.

Moreover, not all of the reforms were as effective as they appeared on paper. Measures such as the Rivers Pollution Act were permissive not mandatory, so that local authorities could evade responsibility for implementing them if they so chose. Disraeli had long disapproved of compulsion, ever since his opposition to the centralising character of the New Poor Law of the Whigs. He explained his thinking in a speech on the Agricultural Tenants Bill

1 Permissive legislation is the characteristic of a free people. It is easy to adopt compulsory legislation when you have to deal with those who only exist to obey; but in a free country, and especially in a country like England, you must trust to persuasion and example as
5 the two great elements, if you wish to effect any great changes in the manners of the people.

Blake points out that by 1880, as a result of this approach, only 10 out of 81 local authorities had implemented the Artisans Dwellings Act. The government was setting down a standard, and progressive local authorities such as Birmingham derived much benefit from the opportunities available; unfortunately, most did not perform so well.

Nonetheless, for most Conservatives the legislation went quite far enough and if Disraeli was to retain their backing he had to recognise their outlook and anxieties. Many of them still believed in *laissez-faire* and felt that government should uphold the rights of private property. Along with many Liberals, they were wary of intervention by the state, and preferred to stress self-reliance and self-improvement rather than collective action by the government on behalf of the community. These attitudes were strengthened in the Conservative Party as a result of its changing social base. The Conservatives were the party of landed property, but in the 1870s many industrialists, factory and coal owners, had sought safe haven within their ranks; they had been frightened away from the Liberal Party by Gladstone's alleged radicalism. The party was now acting in defence of those who owned industrial and commercial property. These men were unlikely to favour measures to tackle social evils, such as long hours, low wages and other poor factory conditions. Such measures would have jeopardised their profits, and alienated their sympathies.

They were aware of the costs that reform might impose. They favoured low taxation, and particularly after 1876 the Chancellor was concerned to restrain expenditure. This limited scope for reform, for most changes in living and working conditions required public finance. This either came from taxes or the rates. As Conservatives often owned larger properties, they were concerned with any increase in their rate burden, and this limited action in areas such as education. In the traditionally Conservative rural areas, there was much alarm about local government expenditure.

These considerations meant that the social reforms passed between 1874 and 1880 were inevitably more modest in scope than might have been expected from a reading of Disraeli's early literature and speeches. Indeed, they were not even mentioned in the 1880 manifesto, which hardly suggests that the leadership attached great significance to them. Foreign policy was seen as far more important. Yet for all the limitations, they formed a worthwhile instalment of measures, ones of a scale and variety which 'root and consolidate a party'. Judged by sheer numbers, the list is impressive, but this, of course, says nothing of the measures' quality or lasting importance. In areas such as health, housing and the trade unions, the legislation was in advance of that of Gladstone, and was potentially of much benefit to those affected. Such considerations probably help to explain the much-quoted observation of one Lib-Lab MP, Alexander MacDonald, who remarked in a letter to *The Times* in 1879 that 'The Conservatives have done more for the working classes in five years than the Liberals have in fifty'.

Disraeli's rhetoric of 1872, if vague in character, was broadly fulfilled, for there had indeed been action to improve the 'conditions of the people'. His broad backing for changes suggests that he appreciated their significance, and his observations to contemporary confidants reflect this understanding. To Lady Bradford, speaking of particular reforms, especially of the Artisans' Dwellings Act, he stressed that they were important, 'because they indicate a policy round which the country can rally'. He was particularly impressed by Cross's labour reforms, for they fitted his conception of change perfectly, in that they did not involve government regulation, imposed no burden on the Exchequer, and, by giving the unions what they wanted, had settled 'the greatest question of the day; the relations between Capital and Labour'. Of the Employers and Workmen Act, he flattered the queen by telling her of his great pleasure that it had been passed on the anniversary of Coronation Day, and remarked that it settled 'the long-envenomed disputes between master and servant'. He thought that it was even more significant than the 1874 Ten Hours measure, 'which had had so beneficial an effect in softening the feelings of the working multitude'.

p) Disraeli and Overseas Policy

Earlier in his career Disraeli had not been an enthusiast for colonies, and had described them as 'millstones around our neck'. As late as 1866, he had written 'Leave the Canadians to defend themselves, recall the African squadron'. Yet in his Crystal Palace speech he had condemned the Liberals for their efforts, 'so continuous, so subtle, supported by so much energy, and carried on with so much ability and acumen, to effect the disintegration of the Empire of England'. By then, he seemed to be a keen advocate of Empire, perhaps seeing it as an issue on which to damage his opponents by impugning their patriotism. Furthermore, at a time when republican sentiment in the country was growing, the cry of Empire might rally people to the Throne as the symbol of an expanding country.

Disraeli's Crystal Palace speech offered little by way of detail, and his ideas on the Empire were generally thrown out somewhat casually and without a clear grasp of the actual issues. Although he is often credited with being the first front-rank British statesman to adopt a definite policy of imperial expansion, his policies do not match the image of him as a committed imperialist. He was little interested in the details of colonial settlement, and often reacted to events as problems arose rather than initiating positive action himself.

His genuine interest was in India and the mysterious Orient. India, with its vast population of over 170 million, was a centre for trade, and an outlet for British goods and a source of valuable imports such as raw cotton, tea and wheat. More than this, it was the 'jewel in the Crown', for it offered the British governing classes a chance to show that they could successfully control native peoples and introduce them to Western ideas of civilisation. Because of this, governing India was a noble mission, and Disraeli was intent on preserving its safety, and the security of all routes to it.

He was able to perceive that a strong British Empire could stand firm in the world against any growing power; the Empire would thus be part of the reassertion of Britain's role and influence in the world. This imperial interest was evident in many events during his premiership, such as the annexation of Fiji, the purchase of the Khedive of Egypt's majority shareholding in the Suez Canal Company, and the annexation of the Transvaal. One of his most typical gestures was that which made the Queen 'Empress of India' in 1876. This was not a new idea, but one to which Gladstone had been noticeably unreceptive. It pleased Victoria, and was an indication of his wish to exalt the standing of an established British institution as well as of the importance he attached to the sub-continent.

His first major biographers, Monypenny and Buckle, discerned a 'genuine interest' in the Empire on Disraeli's part, and spoke of his 'prophetic vision'. Later historians have not been able to substantiate this and have shown his policy in office to be more of a series of improvisations and responses than a clear set of intentions. Fundamentally, he was not interested in the difficulties of particular colonies; what was more important was that these colonies were part of a powerful Empire taking its place in the world.

This was characteristic of Disraeli's entire approach to overseas affairs. Having criticised Gladstone's allegedly inactive and supine policy, he had no very specific ideas of his own. In 1874 he wanted to assert Britain's strength in Europe and in the world. He believed that Britain was isolated and in general decline, and he was determined to enhance Britain's greatness. His approach to questions of overseas policy was in some ways like that of Lord Palmerston; it was a tough, no-nonsense one, and one which was instinctively patriotic.

Disraeli was at the height of his reputation in 1878 on his return from Berlin, where a congress had taken place to resolve the Eastern Question and Russian claims to parts of the Ottoman Empire. He had achieved his aim of bringing about a halt to Russian aggression in the Balkans for the time being, and he had also gained a new acquisition for the British Empire, Cyprus. He came home a popular hero, claiming to have brought back 'peace with honour'.

q) Defeat and Death

If an election had been called in 1878 Disraeli would almost certainly have been victorious, but the government had no reason to call one with two or three more years left before parliament must be dissolved. Over the following months the ministry's difficulties increased and as the time for an election drew nearer the outlook appeared less encouraging. Britain entered into the beginnings of the long depression which was to mark the last two decades of the nineteenth century, and in 1879 high unemployment was a serious problem. Disraeli had no answer to the demands of the Farmers' Alliance for some relief, and when his defeat came in the election he called in 1880 he claimed that 'hard times' had been responsible for undermining the reputation of his administration.

For the Opposition, however, this was not the key issue. Gladstone attacked the government's alleged 'impiety' in its handling of overseas matters, denouncing the failures of a 'forward' policy in the Transvaal' and its actions in Afghanistan. He claimed that Disraeli had 'weakened the Empire by needless wars', and in his Midlothian Campaigns he poured invective upon the conduct of affairs. Disraeli was too old and too weary to answer the attack. He was unable to tour the country to restore enthusiasm. Similarly, his election address, with its warnings about Irish separatist demands, seemed to lack relevance to the immediate situation. Gladstone and the Liberals were more aware of the need to respond to the new electorate at this time, and their organisation was in vigorous fighting shape. By contrast, Conservative organisation was in decline after the improvements of ten years before. The outcome was a decisive defeat, in which the Conservatives lost support throughout the country, except in the South-east.

Disraeli had spent the years since 1876 in the House of Lords where he missed the lively atmosphere of the Lower House. By now, tired, lonely and often impassive, he was described as having 'lustreless eyes and face, like some Hebraic parchment', as he sat alongside Conservative peers. He continued to lead the party until his death in April 1881.

3 Organisational Matters

After the repeal of the Corn Laws, the main institutional elements of the party remained in Peelite hands. RF Bonham, the Principal Agent, and the Chief Whip, Sir John Young, were on Peel's side, and the Party Fund was used to back Peelite candidates. Soon after this, the structure created in the 1830s fell into decline and disuse, as the Peelite forces gradually lost their cohesion. Bonham disappeared from political life.

a) Developments outside the House, 1846-67

The rump of the Conservatives toyed with the idea of a change of name because their title was so closely associated with Peel. They thought of calling themselves Protectionists, but within a few years the label had ceased to be appropriate. The 'Country Party' was a possibility, but the leadership feared that either term might serve as a barrier to would-be recruits. 'Conservative' had a more national appeal, and its continued use seemed to keep the door ajar to the Peelites.

The former Protectionists had to start almost from scratch, for they possessed no organisation and no funds. It is because the party had to be relaunched in 1846 that Lord Blake dates the Conservative Party from this date, for although the name can be traced to the early thirties, the organisation cannot: 'From every aspect of institutional continuity whether as a party within Parliament or outside, 1846 is a better year of birth than 1832 or 1833'.

In 1852 Disraeli decided to put more vigour into the party organisation by appointing a new Chief Whip and reviving the post of Principal Agent. As a result, power was vested with the leadership, the whips and in the Carlton Club until the reforms of two decades later. This was the era in which 'club politics' flourished, for apart from the Carlton Club, situated in Pall Mall, since 1840 there had been the Conservative Club which served as a substitute for those who could not gain entry into the over-subscribed Carlton, and in 1864 a less-exclusive Junior Carlton Club was formed. This catered for what Disraeli called 'the working corpus of our party', by which he meant the professional men, the 'country attorneys and agents who want a political and social focus in London'.

By then, the influence of the Carlton Club had already passed its hey-day, but it was still much used by grandees from the rural constituencies. In the more urban areas, the gentry were less involved in Conservative politics, and often it was a local solicitor who carried out the important task of organising the registration of voters. A new Conservative Registration Association was founded in 1863 to co-ordinate their work.

b) Developments inside the House of Commons, 1846-81

We have already seen that within the House of Commons no party was dominant between 1846 and 1867. There was a tendency for groups to splinter, but broadly there were the Peelites, the Protectionists, the Whigs, the Radicals and the Irish. There was not always a clear line of demarcation between them, and no group could count on the loyalty of its supporters. There was much cross-voting, for party discipline was weak. It required only a few MPs to change their vote, for the government to fall; this gave MPs substantial influence.

Things were different after the 1867 Reform Act. Any government, Liberal or Conservative, knew that if it failed to deliver an appealing programme to the new voters they might prove fickle and switch their allegiance, as happened in 1868, 1874 and 1880. Governments therefore became more concerned to ensure that their policies were likely to please the electorate; they also needed to be sure that they would pass through the House of Commons. This led to an intensification of activities by the party whips, as governments needed to be able to rely on their supporters. The number of 'whipped' divisions in the House grew markedly. Samuel Beer, in *Modern British Politics*, has demonstrated the sharp increase in party unity between the years 1860 and 1881. His figures show that when the whip was applied, on 63 per cent of the votes in 1860 and 87.9 per cent in 1881, at least 90 per cent of MPs 'toed the line'.

After the 1874 election Disraeli sought to keep his backbenchers in line with the policy of the Cabinet and the not-very-specific programme which they had been elected to support. Ministers were expected to set an example, and to vote loyally with the government; any who did not do so were sternly rebuked. As the figures have indicated, most of the backbenchers also went along with the government, though some were worried by the cost of legislative changes and on occasion exhibited a spirit of independence in the lobbies.

c) Developments Outside the House after 1867

After 1867 the idea of branches in the constituencies supporting the parties in the House of Commons received a new impetus, and whereas in the past general elections had often been fought at the local level on matters of purely local concern, this was no longer to be the case. With the vote extended to so many workingmen, parties needed to organise their support. Much of the initiative for this came from the politicians at Westminster who hoped that they would be able to influence and control the new electors so that an age of increasing democracy would not result in the rise of extremism. Gradually, organised activity spread outwards from London into the country, based on the party headquarters co-ordinating the work of many associations.

In 1867 the electorate increased from 1.36m to 2.46m, and the bulk of the additional voters were from the working classes of the towns and cities. The Birmingham Liberals, with much help from the young Joseph Chamberlain, had been quick to see the opportunities created by the Reform Act, but following their successful example many associations were formed by both parties up and down the country. Often they were based on the old Registration Societies. These associations were expected to 'nurse' constituencies between elections and to organise support during them. New techniques of persuasion were required, and this involved a greater emphasis upon explaining policy, via manifestoes and speechmaking tours. Leaflets were handed out and voters were carefully canvassed so that on election day the maximum party vote could be mobilised.

In the case of the Conservatives, in addition to the new associations, several workingmen's organisations were created, places where working-class voters could have a drink and a game of billiards, and make their contribution to local party activity. They were usually clubs rather than associations, and it was the latter which were linked by the National Union of Conservative and Constitutional Associations, set up in 1867. Some people still had doubts about the word 'Conservative', hence the addition to the name, which had the added advantage of seeming to imply that opponents were, by definition, 'unconstitutional'. Altogether, there were spokesmen from 55 constituencies at the meeting which established the National Union, the purpose of which was 'to consider by what organisation we may make Conservative principles effective among the masses'.

The National Union did not seek a say in determining the party programme, and at its 1873 Conference one of its founders stressed that it had been 'organised rather as ... a handmaid to the party, than to usurp the functions of party leadership'. It got off to an inauspicious start. No ministers attended its inaugural gathering and there was some anxiety in the constituency associations that they would lose their identity and independence in this larger creation. It was the arrival of John Gorst as one of its Joint-Secretaries which gave its status and fortunes a boost. He had chaired the meeting in 1867 at which it was launched and had become Party Agent in 1870. He was an industrious and able organiser who had a genuine belief in the concept of the Conservative workingman, and was keen to develop the party's appeal in the urban areas. He saw Disraeli's Tory Democracy as an attractive creed to sell to the new electorate, and Disraeli himself helped him enhance the reputation of the National Union by choosing to make his two big speeches in 1872 at its regional and national conferences.

The Union was the mass organisation which represented the party in the country. New machinery was needed at the centre, in London, to manage the next campaign, so that there could be the best possible back-up for candidates in the field, by way of propaganda, speeches and funds. Conservative Central Office was established in 1870, though it did not acquire this name for another year. It set out to improve the number and quality of candidates, and by 1874 the Conservatives were in fighting shape. Their superior organisation contributed to the scale of their victory, for they were fielding more candidates than they had ever done before and these men were better supported from headquarters.

In 1872 the two new national organisations moved into the same building, and Central Office became a powerful headquarters from which to arrange future party election campaign and to co-ordinate activity in the country. Disraeli's reforms had established the broad pattern of Conservative organisation which exists today - in parliament, the leadership and the Whips; outside, the Conservative headquarters at Central Office and a network of associations around Great Britain.

4 Assessment of the Disraelian Contribution

On Disraeli's death it fell to his arch-rival, Gladstone, to pay tribute to his qualities and his contribution to British political life. Gladstone anguished over his speech. Significantly, he preferred to dwell on some admirable personal qualities - 'his strength of will, his long-sighted consistency of purpose, reaching from his first entrance upon the avenue of life to its very close; his remarkable power of self-government, and last, but not least of all, his great parliamentary courage' - rather than on his policies and achievements. In fact, Gladstone strongly disapproved of Disraeli and felt that he had debased the standard of political life. He saw him as opportunistic, unprincipled and lacking in the ethical sense which he believed to be so important. He could recognise that Disraeli had talents which set him above many other political figures but he objected to the way in which they were used - in such a way as to serve his own ambition and self-interest.

It is hard to deny the element of unscrupulousness and opportunism, traits noted by one of his successors, Lord Salisbury, who as the Earl of Cranborne, had so disliked the Second Reform Act of 1867. He had described him as 'without principles and honesty ... in an age of singularly reckless statesmen, he is I think beyond question the one who is least restrained by fear of scruple'.

Opportunism is a recurring charge in criticisms of Disraeli and the twists and turns of his career - in particular, his exploitation of the issue of protection - provide much evidence to substantiate it. However, some historians have sought evidence of an underlying consistency in his approach to public affairs. In as much as there was one, Lord Blake believes it is to be found in his determination to maintain the position of the landed interest in British life. He quotes a letter Disraeli wrote to Lord Stanley in 1848 in which he describes the task of the official leader of the Conservative Party in the House of Commons as being 'to uphold the aristocratic settlement of the country'. He was referring not just to the great noble families, but to the social hierarchy found throughout rural England, including such bastions of the squirearchy as JPs and other substantial landowners.

Of course, it was among these 'gentlemen of England' that the party had its greatest strength at that time; it was in the county seats and in the small boroughs where the gentry had great influence that the Conservatives picked up most of their seats. Particularly after the Repeal of the Corn Laws, the party was primarily a party of the countryside. That element always remained, so that it is not surprising that Disraeli wished to preserve the 'aristocratic settlement'. However, at that time he was on occasion very dismissive about the squires who made up the parliamentary party, once referring to some who wished to speak in a debate as 'old trash'. Or again, he described some of the Tories soon after as 'destitute of ideas'. The fact is that he needed the landowners;

they were the bulk of his party, and without them he was lost. In as much as he upheld their position, he was ensuring that he had a political future. His was a party of the land, and as Bruce Coleman has written, 'The maintenance of the aristocratic constitution ... and the interests of landownership' were fundamental to mid-century Conservatism. However, Disraeli was prepared to ignore their advice when it seemed expedient to 'dish the Whigs' in 1867.

For all of Disraeli's failings, there is much which makes him appealing. He lacked the *gravitas* of Gladstone, with his deep moral fervour, and found his opponent something of a prig. Gladstone's style and manner can today seem very dated, for he was in many ways a typical Victorian. Disraeli's speeches, for all their classical allusions, can still be read today, and still sound lively. His colourful personality and his flair for self-dramatisation and publicity give him an extra appeal. He did not take himself too seriously, but suspected that the English people, 'being subject to fogs and possessing a large middle class, prefer grave statesmen'.

Disraeli was a fascinating character and the myth that has been woven around him only serves to heighten the interest. Few statesmen have remained so eminent in their reputation or possessed his attraction. He was only at the top of the pole with effective power for six years, and the scale of his achievements in office was good but not remarkable. But at different times he played out interesting roles, the outrageous and reckless adventurer, the tormentor of Peel, the man who claimed to have 'educated' his party, the supreme opportunist of the 1850s and 60s, the aged prime minister finishing his days in the House of Lords. As Robert Rhodes James has observed, 'The deplorable young Disraeli had moved, by careful and deliberate metamorphosis, into the respectable Disraeli, the saviour of the Conservative cause, and [then] into the immortal Lord Beaconsfield'.

His reputation at the end of the nineteenth century was not high, but it was resurrected by Monypenny and Buckle in their multi-volume biography which first appeared in 1910. They were impressed by the Disraelian legacy, seeing him as the advocate of a strong overseas policy based on British interests, the defender of ancient institutions and a reforming Tory Democrat who was concerned to improve living conditions. Thereafter, there were few major assessments until Lord Blake produced his massive and important biography in 1966. Blake was clearly fascinated by his subject, but not uncritical, and ultimately found Disraeli's achievements to be more a matter of his style than of substance.

a) His Reputation Within the Modern Conservative Party

In 1883, on the anniversary of his death, some of his followers wore primroses in their lapels, as a mark of respect. From this gesture, there developed the Primrose League which was formed to spread his ideas and perpetuate his memory. In particular, it aimed to uphold 'religion, the estates of the realm and the imperial ascendancy'. Lord Randolph Churchill was much involved in its early history, and was to become an exponent of Tory Democracy, an elusive idea which was based on Disraelian attitudes and policies. In 1907, John Gorst attempted to define the policy of his former leader, saying,

1 The principle of Tory Democracy is that all government exists solely for the good of the governed ... that all who are entrusted with any public function are trustees not for their own class, but for the nation at large; and that the mass of the people may be trusted
5 so to use the electoral power which should be freely conceded to them, as to support those who are promoting their interests. It is democratic because the welfare of the people is its supreme end; it is Tory because the institutions of the country are the means by which the end is to be attained.

Disraeli, though no modern democrat, would have echoed this spirit of 'Trust the People'. Since Gorst's time, many have placed much emphasis on his contribution to Tory Democracy, and he has become a figure of legend in the Conservative Party. His very name has provoked spontaneous applause from many people at Tory conferences who probably have only the barest acquaintance with what he actually did. They know him to have been a Conservative hero, and mention of his name is a coded way of inviting listeners to bear in mind the 'One Nation' approach. Initially, the Primrose League did much to foster that idea, so that the interests of the working classes were not overlooked. Today, speakers invoke that same viewpoint, to ensure that the party seeks to appeal to all of the people, and does not favour the interests of one group at the expense of another.

In the short run, any progress in the direction of Tory Democracy was very limited, for Churchill's attempts to develop the tradition were swiftly terminated by his resignation in 1886 (see page 126). For several years after, the party's aristocratic old guard remained firmly in control, and Conservative policy lacked the bold Disraelian imprint.

However, in the twentieth century, much folk-lore grew up around his memory, and he has been seen, in *The Conservative Tradition,* as the man responsible for 'that harmonious union, that magnificent concord of all interests, of all classes, on which our national greatness depends'. The Disraelian myth has clearly been a potent one, one which represents how many more progressive Conservatives like to see themselves. He has been credited with a degree of interest in living conditions which he never had, and his efforts at improvement were more spasmodic than Conservatives sometimes suggest. His contribution to Tory Democracy has been exaggerated, and bears only a loose resemblance to the facts of his career. Often, his policies were pursued with a sharp eye to political advantage, and he was always more of a realist than an idealist, knowing what might be acceptable at a given time.

Yet for all of the qualifications, to Conservatives of a later generation he is an inspiration; the more informed look back, unselectively sometimes, on what he wrote and did for justification of their own approach. For those who believe in using the power of the state to tackle social and economic problems, the Disraelian precedent provides a useful example. Several leaders have been keen to deny the idea that they have ever been members of a 'party of unbridled, brutal capitalism'. As a prominent postwar Conservative, Sir Anthony Eden, continued, 'Although we believe in personal responsibility and personal initiative in business, we are not the political children of the laissez-faire school'.

However, it was Stanley Baldwin, the dominant inter-war Conservative, who was particularly fond of quoting Disraeli. He urged his supporters to work towards 'a further period of ordered progress in the tradition of that greatest of our leaders, Lord Beaconsfield.' This was an appropriate comparison for a Conservative leader to pursue in the world of the General Strike, when class conflict was acute. He was calling for a lessening of industrial tension and policies of national harmony, around which people could unite.

For Conservatives ever since, the Disraelian mantle has been one they have wished to assume as they sought to unite the nation by policies of moderate reform and a lessening of social tension. Winston Churchill was able to claim that the acceptance of new policies in the 1950s was in the Tory tradition, and that the welfare state and managed economy were descended from 'the Tory Democracy of Lord Beaconsfield and after him, Lord Randolph Churchill'.

Baldwin, Butler, Macmillan and Heath can also claim descent from him. It was Edward Heath who, in defending the controversial 'Social Charter' of the European Community against its many critics, remarked that 'We Conservatives have possessed a social policy ever since Disraeli'. To advance such a view in the 1980s was less fashionable, for Margaret Thatcher was not seen as a soothing, healing leader; she made little use of the Disraelian legacy, and it was left to the 'wets', her opponents in the party, to make use of the name of perhaps their most-quoted leader.

Disraeli did believe in the need for the Conservative Party to be broad-based in its appeal, and not to be the preserve of a single class. He was wise to recognise that 'the palace is not safe when the cottage is not happy'. His period at the top did give a new dimension to the party image and programme, equipping it with an element of social concern. His rhetoric was impressive, for he was a master of the political phrase, and Tory Democracy conjured up a useful image, the idea of a paternalistic aristocracy which looked after the working classes against the selfish interests of the rising industrial middle classes, just as he had outlined in *Sybil*. However, the actual content of his legislation hardly bears out the description, and as Blake reminded us, it did not really involve a significant new departure in social policy; neither did it have much to do with his earlier philosophy.

Every party has figures from the past whom they regard with special affection. They are useful in that they show the link between modern politicians and those of an earlier period. For the Conservative Party, which prides itself on its roots in the past, they are of particular value, and the names of Pitt, Disraeli and Churchill are ones which still stand out today. Unlike Pitt, Disraeli was proud to call himself a Tory, so that his reputation has not been much disputed; no one in the party needs to justify his claim to a leading place in Conservative history.

b) Peel and Disraeli as Conservative Leaders

It is as a 'One Nation' Disraelian, rather than as a Peelite, that many Conservatives would like to portray themselves. As we have seen (see pages 73-4), Peel's name does not arouse great emotions, and he is less often seen as a party hero. One reason for this is obvious. For all of his good work in recreating the Conservative Party, Peel is seen as the man who by mishandling of the Corn Law issue dealt it a devastating blow which ruined it for a generation. Even though Disraeli was the architect of his fall and played a leading part in opening up that split, his memory shines more brightly. For, although he was defeated in 1880, he left the party in an altogether healthier condition, so that it was in a position to compete on favourable electoral terms and to dominate the period which followed.

Disraeli pursued his aims with more panache, more political skill, and more concern for party unity. However, in some ways the two men's contributions were remarkably similar. Both were in the business of educating their party to new conditions. Peel after 1832 and Disraeli after 1846 were leading a party which was at a low ebb in its fortunes. New vigour and a change of image were essential if survival was to be assured. Both saw the need for the party to adapt and to come to terms with a changing situation.

However, they represented different strands of party tradition. Disraeli found Peelite Conservatism not at all to his liking, for it placed too little emphasis on safeguarding those institutions he so much revered, was not rooted in principle, and was too willing to accommodate itself to change. Moreover, the ideas they propounded were different. Peel was concerned to broaden the party's backing to cater for the new middle classes who had become a dominant force and whom Disraeli much despised. Disraeli's dream, from the time of his Young England days, harked back to an earlier age. He spoke of a party led by a patrician landed element with a sense of duty, which had a care for, and an appeal to, voters in the industrial towns.

As Professor Gash has noted, a curious feature of the Conservative party is that, although its practice has almost invariably been Peelite, in that it developed to become a party of the middle-class men of landed, commercial and industrial property, its myth has been Disraelian. Disraeli imparted the idea that Conservatism, led by a wealthy aristocracy with a sense of concern for the whole nation, could survive into a more democratic age. It need not fear the extension of the franchise. If Tory Cabinets of the twentieth century appear to be Peelite in their composition, the language of many of the party leaders has been based on the Disraelian legacy; respect for ancient institutions allied to an approach which speaks of the broadest national interests, rather than those of their own more wealthy supporters.

Making notes on 'Peel to Disraeli, 1846-81'

Most examination work concentrates on Disraeli's involvement in the events of 1867 and the Second Ministry of 1874-80. Your notes should include sections on;

> Parliamentary Reform; his motives and attitude, the passage of his Bill and its importance
> Disraeli as Opposition leader; policy statements and the revival of party organisation
> The importance of Sir Richard Cross; his approach to social reform
> The main social reforms of the ministry; know 6-7 examples well, on health, housing, factories and unions
> Assessment of the reforms; list their alleged deficiencies
> Foreign andOverseas Policy; interest in Empire, more assertive role
> 1880 election defeat; reasons

At this stage, ask yourself why Disraeli is a character so appealing to modern Conservatives. What is there about his personality and work about which they can enthuse? Make a list of the points you consider important. Have they 'got him right' or do they misunderstand him?

Answering essay questions on 'Peel to Disraeli, 1846-81'

Questions tend to concentrate on Disraeli's work as PM, although infrequently you could be asked how and why he became leader. Therefore to be on the safe side you need to examine the main stages of his early career, particularly his involvement in the events of 1845-6 and 1866-7, and to consider the 'disadvantages' he overcame.
Questions on his ministry mainly fall into three types.

1 You could be asked why he won the election of 1874 and lost six years later, in which case you need to review his work to promote victory in the

first election, and show how and why he lost support prior to the second. Ask yourself whether he had really done enough to win the allegiance of enfranchised working men to the Conservative Party.

2 Most questions are on his work as a reformer. Unless the question is limited to social policy, you should mention his interest in parliamentary reform. You may be asked to compare his reforms with those of Gladstone, but on the 'great ministry' alone you are often invited to endorse the view that he made 'A significant contribution to social reform'. Some questions are more probing, requiring you to think of Disraeli's motives and strategy, as well as assessing the efficacy of his changes. An example of this type of question is: 'Disraeli possessed neither a coherent social policy nor a genuine interest in social problems'. Discuss.

The phrase 'coherent social policy' is a key one, as is the 'genuine interest'. Did he really have a 'social policy', and in the late nineteenth century when laissez-faire was still the order of the day for many people, would any Prime Minister have had a 'coherent' one? Were not his

Tories in Wilderness to 1866	Rise of Disraeli to Real Power	Disraeli in Office 1874-80
1846 Repeal of Corn Laws	1846 Repeal of Corn Laws	1874 Victory
Tory split Peelites: some drift over to Liberals Protectionists	Emergence as leader of Protectionists	Policy of 'Empire, Monarchy and Social Reform'
Protectionists become Conservative Party	Seized chance, 1867, to pass Parliamentary Reform	Package of Social Measures, 1874-6
Derby led Minority Govts 1852 1858-9 1866-8	1868 PM	Assertion of British Interests Abroad
Passage of Parliamentary Reform, 1867	1872 Crystal Palace Speech	1880 Election Defeat
	1874 Election victory	

Summary - From Peel to Disraeli, 1846-81

policies based more on improvisation? The 'genuine interest' is perhaps easier to tackle; think about his attitude in *Sybil,* but also about his approach to particular reforms early and late in his career.

3 Some examiners like to ask about Disraeli's legacy to the party - for example 'What does the Conservative Party owe to the leadership of Disraeli?' - or even to compare his contribution with that of Peel. Consider Disraeli's Tory Democracy. Was it a reality? Did it die with him? Were his achievements ones of style, not substance? How was he regarded by contemporary figures in the party? Why is he still so revered by Tories today?

In tackling a general question on his legacy, you would do well to equip yourself with two or three short, apt quotations. Too many of them lose their impact, and the examiner wants you to think about your own views. Long, half-remembered quotes are similarly not helpful, for it is unclear which point is the one you are really trying to establish. Nonetheless, the occasional, accurately-recalled observation can be useful, perhaps in the introduction to your essay, to help you set out the historical controversy surrounding a particular figure, or in the conclusion, to support your own judgement. You might do well to arm yourself with some useful quotations to assist you in reaching your conclusions on Disraeli; make an accurate note of them.

You should now be in a position to think about the respective approach of Peel and Disraeli to the problems of their day. Write down a paragraph summarising Peelite Conservatism, and another one on the Disraelian variety; would you wish to use the word 'Tory' to describe Disraeli?

Answering source-based questions on 'Peel to Disraeli, 1846-81'

1 Disraeli and *The Times* on the state of the Tory Party
Carefully read the extracts on pages 85 and 89. Answer the following questions.
a)   To what extent do the two sources agree on Disraeli's contribution to the revival of the party? (5 marks)
b)   What were the 'flagrant errors' (page 89, line 7) which Disraeli had weaned the party from? (3 marks)
c)   In the light of his work up to 1860, what evidence is there to substantiate Disraeli's claim that he 'educated his party' from its 'great depression and disorganisation'? (4 marks)
d)   How reliable are the two sources as evidence of Disraeli's contribution? (4 marks)
e)   What other evidence might be useful to someone seeking to give a balanced picture of Disraeli's political effectiveness in this phase of his career? (4 marks)

2 Disraeli's Opposition Speeches, 1872
Carefully read the extracts from the Manchester and Crystal Palace speeches on pages 92 and 93. Answer the following questions.
a)   What were the main charges that Disraeli made against the Liberal administration of Gladstone? (3 marks)
b)   What were the main features of the Conservative programme outlined in the Manchester and Crystal Palace speeches? (5 marks)
c)   In what ways did Disraeli's Crystal Palace speech seek to fulfil his wish to make the party less one of 'exclusiveness and restriction'? (page 93, line 4) (3 marks)
d)   Give examples of the way in which the choice of phraseology and language in the second of the two speeches illustrates Disraeli's desire to widen the appeal of Conservatism. (4 marks)
e)   Re-read the extract from the Tamworth Manifesto (page 54). What were the main similarities and differences between the Conservatism outlined by Peel and Disraeli in the Tamworth Manifesto and in the Manchester and Crystal Palace Speeches? (5 marks)

3 Disraeli and Social Reform
Carefully read the extracts on pages 94, 95 and 99. Answer the following questions.
a)   What was the relationship of the two classes as outlined by Disraeli in *Sybil?* (3 marks)
b)   Why did Disraeli favour 'permissive legislation'? (3 marks)
c)   To what extent and in what ways did permissive legislation and the views represented in the *Fortnightly Review* impede Disraeli's government in fulfilling the aspirations described in *Sybil?* (10 marks)
d)   What criteria should be used to assess the effectiveness of the Disraelian social reforms? (4 marks)

4 Disraeli, the Tory Statesman
Take a look at the portrait on the front cover and the one on page 91, and read the section on his personality, pages 90-2. Then answer the following questions.
a)   Compare the description of the young politician making his Maiden Speech with Disraeli's appearance in the portrait and cartoon. In what ways had he changed? (6 marks)
b)   What was there in his later appearance to suggest that he was a figure who commanded a popular following? (3 marks)
c)   Consider the evidence of the pictures and the description. Was he a figure who could inspire trust? (5 marks)
d)   What qualities do you think made him seem appealing to many politicians and other people who knew him? (6 marks)

CHAPTER 6

Conservatives and Unionists, 1881-1914

1 Introduction

Disraeli's electoral success in 1874 had rescued the Conservative Party and provided it with its first victory in a general election since 1841. After his defeat six years later Conservatism did not appear to be well-placed for it had lost its appeal to the voters. Yet by December 1885 the Conservatives were on the verge of a long era of ascendancy. For 20 years they were to have a virtual monopoly of office, winning three out of the four elections, before they were soundly beaten in 1906. The Opposition was condemned to 18 years of parliamentary impotence and internal conflict.

The two decades of Conservative majorities had much to do with the impact of the Irish Question, for it was the issue of Home Rule for Ireland which inflicted such heavy damage on the Liberals' fortunes. The policy lacked attraction for English voters and provoked the break-up of the Gladstonian Party. Liberals such as Joseph Chamberlain and Lord Hartington seceded from their former party and Liberal Unionists increasingly came to be identified with the Conservatives. The coalition of conservative forces opposed to Home Rule (the Conservatives and Liberal breakaways) became the Unionists, though a formal merger did not come about until the organisational reforms of 1911, when the title Conservative and Unionist Party was adopted.

For many people Ireland was the issue which transcended all others in importance. It was primarily the reason why an inveterate former Radical like Chamberlain could find himself on the same side of the political fence as the aristocratic Lord Salisbury, whom he had formerly so vehemently denounced. To Chamberlain, the new division in politics was clear:

1 I am, and shall be in the future, proud to call myself a Unionist, and be satisfied with that title alone, believing it is a wider and nobler title than either of Conservative or Liberal, since it includes them both - since it includes all men who are determined to
5 maintain an undivided Empire, and who are ready to promote the welfare and the union not of one class but of all classes of the community.

There were other factors at work. Gladstone's alleged radicalism, not just over Home Rule, had frightened some of the middle classes into joining with their opponents, for the Conservatives seemed to offer a sturdier defence of the rights of property. This added to Conservative wealth, and the Conservative Party became adept at using its funds to reduce the opposition vote in elections. Voters still had to be registered, and sympathetic barristers were skilled at finding reasons for denying the franchise to likely opponents. The Conservatives could also afford to develop an organisation which maximised the Unionist vote now that the vast majority of men qualified. An effort was made through the Primrose League to arouse greater interest, and in inspiring leaflets such as *What the Conservatives have done for the British People,* much emphasis was placed on Conservative social reforms said to have been good for working men. The record of Disraeli seemed to add some weight to the claim, the more so as the Liberals had not been active in this area.

A weak and divided opposition has often been good for the right-wing cause in British politics, and the Liberals were seriously split after 1886. On issues other than Home Rule, different tendencies appeared in a party which still embraced coal owners as well as coal miners, and factory owners as well as factory operatives. Many Liberals had their own 'fads'. For some, it was temperance, which really meant abstinence from strong drink, for others, it was Welsh Disestablishment. There were Liberal Imperialists and those like Lloyd George who were strongly opposed to imperial expansion. When the Boer War broke out in 1899 it exacerbated these divisions. A year later Lord Salisbury seized the initiative to call the Khaki election in which the Unionists exploited the patriotism of working men, and won handsomely.

Yet if the election of 1900 was the peak of Unionist electoral achievement, the war which made it possible sowed the seeds of Conservative decline. The delay in subduing the Boers dented the mood of euphoria over Empire, and did much to quell patriotic fervour. However, above all, it was Chamberlain's policy of Tariff Reform which aimed to bind the countries of the Empire together, which was so damaging to the Unionists, and it was their turn to split now. As Peel had once divided them over the Corn Laws, now it was Chamberlain who did so over Protection, and in so doing he contributed significantly to Conservative difficulties and Liberal resurgence. In 1906 the Conservatives were reduced to a rump of 132 MPs, supported by 25 Liberal Unionists.

Between 1906 and 1914 the party relied on the House of Lords to maintain its pre-eminence. Balfour, its leader from 1902-11, decided that 'The two Houses shall not work as two separate armies, but shall co-operate in a common plan of campaign ... The real discussion ... is not now in this House [of Commons] ... the real discussion must be elsewhere'. The mood of the party in this period was aggressive. It regarded itself as the rightful party of government, and did not make the necessary adjustment to its reduced influence. It was not particularly choosy about the tactics it adopted, and this was an era described even by several pro-Conservative writers as the one when the Conservatives lost their collective good sense. Their electoral fortunes improved in

1910, but there was little evidence in 1914 that the Conservatives were ready again for office.

2 Personalities and Policies

On Disraeli's death the Conservative Party was led in the House of Commons by Sir Stafford Northcote and in the Lords by Lord Salisbury. From the beginning, the leadership was a cause of dispute. Northcote was prosy and ineffectual, and no match for Gladstone. Several Conservatives wanted to see a more dynamic attack upon the Liberal government. They saw Northcote as too cautious and responsible, and they disliked his excessive gentility. He was a figure of fun, much mocked for his high-pitched voice. Among his more unsparing and persistent critics was Lord Randolph Churchill, who in private mocked him as 'The Goat', on account of the shape of his head, or as the 'GOW', the Grand Old Woman, as opposed to Gladstone who was the Grand Old Man.

a) Lord Randolph Churchill

Lord Randolph Churchill had entered the House of Commons in 1874 as the Conservative MP for the family borough of Woodstock. He came from a privileged background, born at Blenheim Palace, the son of the seventh Duke of Marlborough. He was educated at Eton and Oxford. In the House he aroused the curiosity and admiration of those around him. As a politician, he was well-equipped, possessing boundless self-confidence, a colourful personality, and a brilliant debating style. Slight in build, he was to become a giant among parliamentarians. He was irrepressible and audacious, specialising in a satirical oratorical style. He devastatingly used his wit to savage the Gladstone administration on several fronts, notably the government's handling of Irish affairs and Egyptian policy.

He was also a regular critic of his own party's leadership, and frequently overshadowed the Tories on his own Front Bench. He wanted them to assault Gladstone with more vigour and boldness, but above all he wished to rally his supporters and turn Conservatism into a popular movement. Within the House, he and three others formed themselves into a 'ginger group' which often took a bold and independent line. The four men devoted much of their time to taunting and embarrassing Gladstone, but they also advanced their own creed of Tory Democracy. It had far more appeal than the policies pursued by the Front Bench which seemed to be devoid of ideas and inspiration.

When a member of the House stated that 'There are two great parties in the state', it was Parnell, the leader of those Irish MPs who wanted Home Rule, who shouted out 'Three', thereby prompting Churchill to cap this with 'Four'. The label caught on, for many contemporaries recognised that those in the group did behave as an independent force. Throughout the life of the Liberal ministry their destructive talents were used to goad their own Front Benchers as much as those on the opposite side. The witty, irreverent and half-conspiratorial appeal of the Fourth Party has been compared to that of the Young England group of which Disraeli had been such a prominent member. Both groups disliked the leaders of the party, and whilst the one advocated a radical Toryism the other stressed the need for democratic Conservatism. Neither much liked the consensual approach, as represented by Peel and Northcote.

b) Tory Democracy

Churchill's involvement established his reputation as a Conservative with a future, but his attention was not limited to the House of Commons; neither was his popularity. He wished to see Conservatism develop as a popular movement in the country, and to this end he was prominent in the formation of the Primrose League in 1883, and in attempts to democratise the organisation of the Tory Party (see page 143). He sought to invest the Disraelian concept of Tory Democracy with meaning and substance. However, his observations were rarely very helpful in amplifying it. In 1884 he made the classic non-statement that

ATHWART THE COURSE.

R. Nd-LPH Churchill, in approaching Boat. "IN THE WAY AGAIN! 'OORAY!!"

Athwart the Course, Punch *cartoon, 1883*

'Tory Democracy is a democracy which supports the Tory Party'.

He had elaborated his views a little more lucidly a year earlier in the *Fortnightly Review*, when he had clearly placed himself in the Disraelian tradition, claiming that Tory Democracy was a direct descendant of *Sanitas sanitatum, omnia sanitas*. He saw the Toryism of the 1870s as being 'a scheme of social progress and reform, of dimensions so large and widespreading that many volumes would not suffice to explain its details'. He wished to continue that tradition, and as a great coiner of popular phrases, was able to attract attention. The phrases sounded impressive, but the content was often unclear, and Tory Democracy remains vague and elusive despite his attempted explanation.

He possessed general ideas on policy but they did not amount to a comprehensive programme. The nearest he came to setting one out was to be in his Dartford Speech in 1886. His proposals included land reform to benefit the recently-enfranchised agricultural labourer, including measures to change the agricultural rating system and cheapen the costs of land transfer. He also favoured a reconstruction of local government in the counties, changes in parliamentary procedures and economy in government expenditure so that taxation could be reduced. As a Conservative he was not in a position to propagate bold and expensive social reforms, for these would have seemed threatening to the pockets and property of those members of the upper and middle classes, whose support the party needed to retain. On the one hand, he had to appeal to the aspirations of the conservative middle classes, and on the other to the instincts of the working classes for reform. It was a difficult balancing act for a reforming Tory.

What Churchill lacked was a new economic policy. In the Liberal Party, Chamberlain and fellow Radicals in the early 1880s could win votes by denouncing landlordism, from which they were economically independent. As Lord Blake has observed, there was no comparable interest of which the Conservatives could make a scapegoat. Both landlords and big business had too strong a hold in the Conservative Party. Perhaps the best tactics would have been to think in terms of social insurance on the Bismarckian model, but the Conservatives showed no understanding of such a policy. 'Tory Democracy' remained a fine phrase and not a policy, for Churchill was unable to think outside of his own class even when the exigencies of the party struggle made this desirable. It was neither a realistic doctrine, nor a carefully thought out programme of reform. Indeed, to Lord Rosebery, a Liberal opponent, it was an 'imposture'.

Yet Churchill's speeches and actions were a tonic to the demoralised Tories and, ultimately, it is not for its content but rather for its understanding of the need to be popular that the Tory Democracy of the Fourth Party is remembered. Lady Gwendoline Cecil, the daughter of Lord Salisbury, understood this well. She observed that Churchill saw the necessity for a popular variety of Conservatism, and the need for the party to communicate its ideas: 'It was not the creed of Conservatism that they doubted, but its power of appeal to the electorate'.

Churchill often spoke of the 'traditional institutions' of the country, just as Disraeli had done, but he found it impossible to explain how their survival would enhance the welfare of the people. In another headline-catching phrase, he wanted to 'Trust the People', in the expectation that that they would place their trust in such 'natural rulers' as himself. He emphasised that this had long been part of his philosophy, and that his purpose was; 'To rally the people round the Throne, to unite the Throne with the people, a loyal Throne and a patriotic people, that is our policy and that is our faith.'

Quoting another Churchill observation - when in a cynical and flippant aside he described Tory Democracy as 'mostly opportunism' - Blake concludes that, '[his] position really depended less on any policy or programme than on brilliant opposition demagoguery'. His career, like that of the Fourth Party which he dominated, was to be brief and dazzling. His ultimate purpose was to launch a bid for the leadership, but he underestimated the power of resistance of the Old Guard as represented by Lord Salisbury.

c) Lord Salisbury, his Personality and Qualities

Lord Salisbury was officially declared Conservative leader in 1885 when he formed his first administration. He remained in that position until 1902, yet despite the longevity of his period at the head of his party, including three spells as Prime Minister, his impact on the Conservative Party and its evolution was not very great. Whereas Disraeli achieved a lasting place in Conservative affection, and Lord Randolph Churchill achieved fame (or notoriety) in a career which was over almost before it had begun, Lord Salisbury has left no striking memorial - despite being, in Winston Churchill's words, 'venerable, august Lord Salisbury, Prime Minister since God knows when'. He did little to arouse popular enthusiasm and probably had no wish so to do. For much of his period in office he was carried by events rather than being in control of them.

The other two men were picturesque personalities, whereas Salisbury lacked the attributes needed to become a popular leader. Neither did he command the moral authority of a Gladstone. His was a dignified presence, instantly recognisable by his beard, and if he lacked both eloquence and personal magnetism, he could nonetheless speak effectively when roused by the issues which Gladstone took up. He managed to speak on 70 public platforms between 1880 and 1886.

He was an aristocrat living in a democratic age. Yet he was also a realist with a fine intelligence and a tremendous sense of public duty. He remained aloof and regarded life's successes and failures with a cynical detachment. To him man's journey often seemed an improbable one, and he was unsure to what end it was directed. He believed that as long as one did one's duty the responsibility for the result rested with God.

He held firm views on issues of political principle, and he disliked the extension of the franchise. As Lord Cranborne he had opposed Disraeli in 1867, advancing the view that 'First-rate men will not canvass mobs, and mobs will not elect first class men'. He was frankly sceptical of democracy, and given his negative approach and reactionary views it does seem strange that he should have been Prime Minister for so long. Of course, it is probable that he would not have been so but for the schism over Home Rule which caused the Liberal Party to disintegrate. Yet he was also a realist, with sufficient political good sense to accept the inevitable and to make the best of it. Although he often opposed changes which he thought were unwise, he accepted them once they had been implemented.

In some respects, his personality was not without appeal. Despite his background he disliked upper-class society, even though he could be a charming host. He despised much of the superficiality and shallowness of its members, and was scornful of the sham of the world he inhabited. Yet he was resigned to his fate, for the 'usual destiny of us unfortunate white slaves' was to be 'stressed and bored at dinners and at parties'. He was by preference a solitary man, and resented the effort of society to interfere with his privacy. He loved to play with mechanical contrivances, particularly the telephone, and was known to startle his house guests by unexpectedly calling 'Hey, diddle diddle' down the line - just as he was by suddenly switching out the lights, a new ploy made possible by the coming of electricity.

He was undoubtedly a keen Christian, but mixed up with his religious convictions was a blend of cynicism and fatalism. He was a devout Anglican, and the Church of England had his unswerving loyalty. But his views were not of the sort to appeal to those who liked their religion to be clear-cut and uncomplicated, and his daughter observed that throughout his life he found it hard to accept the moral teaching of the Gospels. He experienced difficulty in fathoming life's meaning - 'God is all-powerful and God is all-loving - and the world is what it is! How are you going to explain that?'.

d) Salisbury and Social Change

Salisbury believed in the traditional, early nineteenth-century 'Church and King' Toryism. He believed that existing institutions should be changed only as far as was necessary to remedy proven deficiencies. Like Burke, he doubted the value of legislation based on planning for the future, for 'Large conceptions in law-making are characterised by their disregard of justice and individual liberty, or their sacrifice of realities to the symmetry of cherished theories'.

For him, the primary business of government was to administer the existing order, and the Conservatives owed their first duty to the classes who relied upon them to defend their interests. He was 'anxious to make this country more pleasant to live in for the vast majority of those who live in it ... [and to] diminish the divergences between classes'. In a general sense, therefore, he was keen on the idea of better living conditions, particularly in housing and the provision of free education. However, such proposals as he made for social reforms were limited by the firm conviction that it was essential to respect private property and do nothing which would weaken self-reliance.

He had little faith in the idea of betterment by legislation, and doubted the power of political action to improve the world. The things that were wrong in life were primarily faults of human nature, and there was little the politicians could do to make men and women better. He had a sombre distrust of any notion of social and economic change. For years, he had battled to check the advance of democracy, and shortly after the great defeat of 1867, he became worried about the advance of socialism, which he described as 'a decorous form of pillage'. He was worried about the future and the threat posed by this and other creeds which threatened the stability of society as it had long been known. He believed that socialists were motivated not by 'a philanthropic spirit, but by a mere impulse of class antipathy'.

He was described in 1892 as the 'Prime Minister of despair whose plan was to accept as inevitable whatever system he found existing', and it was true that he had spent much of his political life fending off change. When explaining his party's attitude to the abolition of church rates, he spoke of what had been gained by the approach he had adopted, 'Even if the Tories are defeated, at any rate, we have obtained delay, and delay is life'. His fears were less intense later in his life, and the Disraeli premiership had shown what could be achieved by a Conservative leader. The image of Conservatism as a national creed, appealing to all sections of the community, had an attraction, as long as achieving this did not involve such an active role for the state that individual liberty was in jeopardy.

e) Home Affairs: The Politics of 1885-6

On the fall of Gladstone's second administration in June 1885 Lord Salisbury agreed to form a minority government. He was at first reluctant for he knew that his position would be perilous with a few months to run in a 'hostile but dying' session of parliament. Nevertheless, with his backbenchers keen for office, he formed what Chamberlain disparagingly called 'the Ministry of Caretakers'. Little of significance occurred, other than the efforts of Lord Carnarvon, the new Viceroy of Ireland, to do a deal with Parnell. Carnarvon favoured a conciliatory approach to Irish problems, and was willing to offer some form of limited self-government. Churchill also wanted a generous settlement, although like Salisbury he was opposed to Home Rule.

However, enough progress in the talks was made to convince Parnell that he could extract more from the Conservatives than from the Liberals. This led him to advise Irish voters in England to vote for Conservative candidates in the November general election. The outcome of polling was a deadlock, in which the 86 Parnellites held the balance. They kept the Conservatives in office, and Salisbury remained as Prime Minister.

Events took a dramatic turn when it became known in mid-December that Gladstone was in favour of Home Rule. His son, Herbert, revealed this information to the press, and alignments on the issue soon became clear-cut. In Salisbury's words, what had been a chimera now became a blazing issue. The Liberals became identified with Home Rule, although among prominent members of the party Chamberlain and Hartington were clearly hostile. The Conservatives viewed the prospect of Liberal disunity with glee. They came out in opposition, and Churchill began to exploit the Ulster question. He knew that the Protestants of the northern counties would never put up with becoming a minority in a predominantly Catholic Irish parliament.

As for Parnell, it became clear that he had miscalculated. It was now apparent that it was the Liberals, not the Conservatives, who were willing to recognise the aspirations of Irish people to govern themselves. His supporters combined with the Liberal opposition to bring down the Salisbury government in January 1886, and Gladstone again became Prime Minister. His intention was to produce a Home Rule Bill, and although Chamberlain joined the new government he soon resigned when the details of the Bill became known to the Cabinet.

Chamberlain led the opposition in the House of Commons. He saw the measure as being 'tantamount to the break-up of the United Kingdom', for he believed that Home Rule would lead to independence. Conservatives shared his fears, and one of their pamphlets denounced Home Rule as a 'direct attack upon England and the English race'. Churchill was in the forefront of their attack. He warned that the Protestant Ulstermen of the northern counties would not accept domination by the Catholics who would out-number them in an Irish parliament, saying 'Ulster will fight, and Ulster will be right'.

The Bill was defeated in the House of Commons by 30 votes as a result of the revolt by 93 dissident Liberals, including Hartington and Chamberlain, who were known as Liberal Unionists. Their decision to vote against the Bill and bring down the government was made easier by the Conservative pledge not to oppose in the next election any Liberal MP who rebelled against the Gladstonian leadership. At this stage, there seemed little enthusiasm for any formal alliance between the two sides, and in the election which followed the government's defeat they fought separate campaigns. The Liberal Unionists, with 78 seats, held the balance in the new House, and generally gave their backing to what was an exclusively Conservative administration in its composition.

f) Salisbury's Second Administration, 1886-92

The early months of Lord Salisbury's government were dominated by the clash between Churchill and the Prime Minister. Churchill had served in the brief ministry of 1885. As the Secretary of State for India he had shown an impressive mastery of detail and a capacity for hard work. Because of his performance and reputation he was an obvious candidate for high office when the Conservatives came back into office. He was appointed as Chancellor of the Exchequer, the youngest since Pitt, a post he combined with that of Leader of the House of Commons. From the beginning he proved to be a difficult colleague to work with as he was so unwilling to compromise.

It was inevitable that the views of the leader and those of Churchill should prove to be a cause of disharmony, for Churchill favoured a more vigorous approach to reform. He did not want the state merely to tinker with the established order of things. However, for a while, Salisbury hoped that his colleague was, underneath the veneer of a radical platform orator, at heart a traditional Conservative, and he treated him with some indulgence. Churchill was impatient for change, and the gulf between the two men widened. The Prime Minister was clearly irritated by the difficulties he encountered because of his ambitious colleague, and explained his tactics in a letter to Lord Cranbrook who had expressed his dismay at the way in which Salisbury was leaning over backwards to accommodate the Chancellor's feelings.

1 What you call my self-renunciation is merely an effort to deal with an abnormal and very difficult state of things. It arises from the peculiarities of Churchill ... [he] is the only possible leader in the House of Commons - and his ability is unquestionable. But he is
5 wholly out of sympathy with the rest of the Cabinet ... Like you, I am penetrated with a sense of the danger which the collapse of the Government would bring about; otherwise I should not have undertaken ... the task of leading an orchestra in which the first fiddle plays one tune and everybody else, including myself, wishes
10 to play another.

The difficulties were political as well as personal, for they represented a divergent view of the nature of Toryism in a democratic age. Salisbury urged caution and wanted to keep the party together. Churchill felt frustrated, and in his Dartford Speech had proposed bold measures which he thought the party should take up. By early November 1886 Churchill's wayward, maverick personality and behaviour were wearying Salisbury, while Churchill was disillusioned that his Dartford programme was in danger of 'falling to pieces'. He believed that the Tories were proving 'incapable of reform', and he wrote to the Prime Minister to express his dismay:

1 I am afraid it is an idle schoolboy's dream to suppose that Tories
can legislate - as I did - stupidly. They can govern and make wars,
and increase taxation and expenditure *a merveille,* but legislation is
not their province in a democratic constitution ... I certainly have
5 not the courage to go on struggling against cliques as poor Dizzy
did all his life.

Salisbury's response is indicative of a very different approach. He
believed in 'the art of the possible', and tried to emphasise this slower,
more cautious and sceptical view of the nature of political change. His
comments also reveal an intuitive insight into the workings of the
Conservative Party.

1 The Tory Party is composed of varying elements, and there is
merely trouble and vexation of spirit in trying to make them work
together. I think the 'classes and dependents of class' are the
strongest ingredients in our composition, but we have so to
5 conduct our legislation that we shall give some satisfaction to both
classes and masses. This is specially difficult with the classes -
because all legislation is rather unwelcome to them, as tending to
disturb a state of things with which they are satisfied. It is evident,
therefore, that we must work at less speed and at a lower
10 temperature than our opponents. Our Bills must be tentative and
cautious, not sweeping and dramatic.

Soon afterwards Churchill ceased to be a problem. He presented the
Cabinet with his Budget proposals, involving increases in death duties
and cuts in military expenditure, in order to bring about reductions in
personal taxation. The rest of his colleagues were unimpressed, and
would not accept his plans. He impulsively resigned. Salisbury willingly
accepted his departure, in Churchill's words, 'like a dog at a bone', and
replaced him as Chancellor with Goschen, a Liberal Unionist. This was
to be the end of Churchill's ministerial career, and he was shortly struck
down with a debilitating disease - probably a venereal one which he had
contracted earlier in his colourful life. He devoted more and more time
to the turf, and in the House his rare speeches were increasingly difficult
to comprehend. He died in 1895.

Why did Churchill resign without putting up more of a fight? Perhaps
he expected that his resignation would lead to the break-up of the
government, or that it would be followed by his reinstatement, amidst
popular acclaim. If this was the case, like many people, he overestimated
his own importance. He was not indispensable, and though he had
received popular backing in 1884 (see page 143) this time his support
ebbed away with 'pathetic rapidity'. There was always someone else. In
his own words, 'I forgot Goschen'.

Then again, perhaps he had had enough. He was out of sympathy with the style and approach of most other ministers, and was a rather solitary figure in the party. Many Conservatives and Liberals regarded him as the 'incarnation of evil, a reckless and insolent iconoclast ... unscrupulous, violent, unprincipled ... one who, to serve the personal ambition which was his sole motive, would stick at nothing'. Those were the words of Lord Rosebery, a Liberal who watched his performance from the other side of the House, and if the judgement is rather too severe and unbalanced, it highlights the way in which many contemporaries thought of him. Having so little parliamentary or Cabinet support, perhaps the rejection of his proposals was just one rebuff too many. He knew that he and other ministers were in disagreement over many issues, and that, besides disputes on particular policies, there was a more general discord over the future direction of the party and the tempo of change.

If he did hope to survive his startling resignation, he chose the wrong time and the wrong issue. The timing was particularly poor, - over Christmas when parliament was not in session. No one was likely to mobilise a campaign on his behalf amidst the seasonal festivities, as a skilful politician with sensitive antennae would surely have known. The issue was also not a crucial one, for economies could probably have been made in other departments, and did not have to come from the military, even though that was his clear preference.

g) Joseph Chamberlain and the Liberal Unionists

The Liberal split over Home Rule had left Lord Hartington and Joseph Chamberlain as Liberal Unionists in the political wilderness. They were unlikely bedfellows, possessing very different personalities and ideas. Hartington was perhaps the last great Whig patrician to play an active role in English politics. His seeming indolence and inertia, his distaste for popular politics and legislation, and his innate caution were in marked contrast to Chamberlain's approach. Chamberlain had made his reputation as a hard-hitting Radical. He had been a reforming mayor of Birmingham (1873-6), and was noted for his drive and determination to get things done. He possessed a flair for party organisation and was prominent in the Liberal 'caucus'. This term, literally meaning a 'meeting of wirepullers', was the one used by critics of the Birmingham Liberal Federation, of which Chamberlain was a prominent member. They disliked his alleged 'Americanisation' of political activity, and his professional approach to canvassing supporters and setting out programmes.

His programme of speech-making around the country culminated in the publication of his Unauthorised Programme of 1885. In it he suggested a policy of land reform, to provide allotments and smallholdings for the benefit of agricultural labourers, graduated income tax, local government reform and free elementary education.

The vehemence of his attacks on those who opposed his approach roused them to fury. He portrayed Lord Hartington and the Whigs as a barrier to achieving his social aims. On the other side, Lord Salisbury and the Conservatives were denounced for their selfish defence of their class interests, 'the class who toil not, neither do they spin'. For many within both parties Chamberlain was too inflammatory, his language going 'too far'. They saw him as a demagogue promoting class warfare.

It was the publication of Gladstone's Home Rule Bill (see page 124) which provoked Chamberlain's opposition to official Liberal policy, and he and Hartington now found themselves fighting on the same side. However, they were temporarily consigned to the political sidelines, particularly after the failure of the Round Table talks in 1887 which were designed to bring about a Liberal reunion.

By an irony of history Chamberlain now became drawn to the Conservative Party which he had spent his life denouncing. He was to spend the next 20 years of his stormy career in close co-operation with its leaders. Perhaps this was not totally surprising because in the mid-1870s he had found that he could work well with some of the Conservative ministers, particularly Cross, and he became convinced that Conservative philosophy could accommodate his social reforming views more easily than the Liberalism of Gladstone. Moreover, he began to develop close personal contacts with Conservatives, and found some of them congenial. In the cause of Empire he discovered an outlet for his ambitions which could be married to their preoccupations. His involvement with the Conservative Front Bench, especially Balfour, steadily developed after 1886, and Salisbury was willing to keep the Liberal Unionists informed of his government's intentions, and was ready to listen to their proposals.

By 1889 he was sharing a platform with Lord Salisbury, and found that he could work with him because the question of Ireland was overriding, far more important than any other issue. Chamberlain never completely abandoned his radicalism, and his commitment to social reform was the inspiration of his attitude to the Empire and Tariff Reform. Inevitably, opportunities within the Conservative Party for him to achieve this goal were slim. Yet his judicious combination of Empire and Social Reform did much to help him retain the loyalty of the working class in Birmingham, and it was his considerable achievement that he could carry the people of Birmingham with him despite his defection to the Conservative cause. The Chamberlains continued to dominate local politics until the end of our period.

h) The Conservatives and Social Reform

Salisbury doubted whether anything useful could be achieved by state action in the field of social improvement, for he believed that the faults within society primarily arose from man's individual failings rather than some more generally treatable condition. Therefore, he had no wish to see his government pursue an actively reformist policy. He preferred instead to place the emphasis upon sound administration of the existing order. Nonetheless, his earlier fears about society had not yet been realised. The enlargement of the franchise had not produced mass anarchy, and though he was still anxious about 'dangerous' new forces such as socialism and the 'vast conflicts' which threatened the nation, he accepted that Conservatism need not be purely about resistance to improvement and the preservation of the status quo. Disraeli had endeavoured to make the Conservative Party one of national appeal, and limited change was acceptable if it furthered this end, whilst at the same time, did not threaten private property and individual rights.

Salisbury was, by preference, a believer in *laissez-faire*, but he felt some compassion for the poor and wished to ease their burdens a little. Such an approach made possible some limited and judicious reforms which would be beneficial to the lot of the working classes. He had, for instance, shown some interest in the problems of their housing in the early 1880s, and was later to legislate to remove some of its most unsatisfactory features in 1885 and 1890.

Most of those who believed in the Tory Democracy of Disraeli had passed from the scene by the mid 1880s, so that the era of improved trade union rights, factory reform and advancements in public health was at an end. Those who took over the reins shared the Salisbury preference for 'good administration', for other than Churchill, in the early months, they were also concerned with issues such as militancy in the unions and the perils of any further movement towards democracy. They therefore also favoured cautious, worthwhile measures, which might bring some credit to the government's reputation. Sometimes the case for reform seemed to be a strong one, for a careful concession made at the right time could forestall a more sweeping measure from their opponents, when they next assumed office. Other causes were taken up when it was no longer easy to evade them.

The most effective reformer was Ritchie at the Local Government Board. He was a businessman, a minister rather in the mould of Sir Richard Cross. Like him, he proved to be a notable legislator, even if his reputation is rather less well-established. He was not a popular politician as Chamberlain and Churchill were, but in a quiet, workmanlike way he sponsored measures in whichever department he was placed. He was responsible for the Local Government (County Councils) Act of 1888. Salisbury anticipated that a Liberal government would ultimately adopt a more radical measure than anything he was prepared to contemplate. Because of this, he set aside his own preference for a cheaper system of indirect elections, and agreed to the scheme that Chamberlain was urging and which Ritchie also favoured. This set aside the rule of the Justices of the Peace, and replaced it with government by 62 directly-elected county councils, elected by the ratepayers. Towns of over 50,000 qualified for County Borough status, which gave them the same powers within their boundaries as the counties were granted. In view of its size, London received County Council status, and in his later ministry (1895-1902), Salisbury presided over the creation of a second tier of 28 London boroughs in 1899.

The Education Act of 1891 was another measure which Chamberlain was urging upon the government, with support from Balfour. It introduced free elementary education, for Salisbury accepted that once the state had made education compulsory it was only fair that there should be no financial burden on parents. Otherwise, he was unsympathetic to matters of popular education, which removed the opportunity for children to be at work and provide cheaper labour for the manufacturers. The government did introduce the Technical Instruction Act of 1889 which allowed local authorities to levy a penny in the £ rate for the purposes of providing technical education. The provision of such a skill was seen as beneficial both to those who received it and to their employers.

There were other measures, though most were of limited importance. The Allotments Acts encouraged local authorities to make land available for rural labourers for allotments and small-holdings. The Tithes Act placed the responsibility for paying the unpopular tax on owners rather than occupiers of land, thereby ending a cause for some resentment, In addition, there were measures dealing with the hours of workers in shops and factories.

In Salisbury's third administration (1896-1902) reforms were few. In 1896 ministers tried to pass an Education Bill and a measure on agricultural rating, but dropped them for the session in the face of opposition in the House and outside. The Education Act of the following year was a much more modest measure to increase the state grant to the Voluntary schools, which primarily meant assisting the Church of England and Catholic schools. A measure to allow for derating of agricultural property did pass in 1897, much to Salisbury's pleasure, but in that year the most important measure was the Workmen's Compensation Act, piloted through the House by Joseph Chamberlain. Workers in several industries who received an injury in the course of their employment could now claim compensation from their employers. To some Conservatives, this was 'revolutionary', but Salisbury was prepared to back Chamberlain, having in 1895 committed this government to a more active social policy 'to ameliorate the conditions of the people' and bring about an 'improvement of the daily life of struggling millions'.

Chamberlain would have liked to see the government introduce Old Age Pensions to reduce pauperism among the elderly. The Germans had gone in for such a policy, and there was growing support in Britain for legislation. Chamberlain was the first leading politician to produce an actual scheme, and it may be that but for the outbreak of the Boer

War something could have been achieved. Salisbury approved in principle a contributory scheme in which the state could establish the machinery, but not be faced with a serious financial burden. Once war broke out, such reforming proposals were shelved.

The legislative achievement of the Salisbury years was modest, although not without value. Certainly there was no spate of bold reforms, but this was only to be expected. After Disraeli's passing the party was content with steady government, and accepted that the first task of ministers was to maintain the existing order. Salisbury's Conservatism was primarily defensive in character, concerned with protecting individual liberty and property, and this was what many of his party wanted. Improvements cost money, and the backbenchers were unhappy at the prospect of higher taxation or excessive burdens being placed on the rates. They welcomed the sort of policy which Salisbury had put to the voters in the 1892 election campaign. It promised to keep costs down. Little mention was made of social reform, and the emphasis was more upon the ability of the party to provide administration of superior competence to the Liberals.

Overall, the Salisbury approach made for what one writer has called 'hesitant benevolence', doing good where this was not threatening to the individuals who hoped the Conservatives would look after them. Such an approach offered little to the working man in the towns, who might have preferred greater recognition of his rights, but the agricultural worker was less neglected. This was because this class had been given the vote in 1884, and both parties were looking for ways to attract the support of agricultural labourers, just as they had sought to do for the urban working man in the years of 1868-80. Moreover, in the 'Great Depression' of the 1880s, there was an obvious need to seek to relieve the lot of those who suffered from its worst effects, and in parts of the countryside its impact was serious.

Social reform in the period 1886-1902 generally reflected the views of the Conservative Prime Minister. Salisbury did not like the idea of 'programmatic politics', the notion that there was a series of commitments to be honoured. Individual measures were taken because they were desirable in themselves, given the condition of the country.

i) The Conservatives and Ireland

For the Conservatives, supported by the Liberal Unionists, the answer to Irish problems was a combination of stern government tempered by reform. The policy was applied by the new Irish Secretary, Salisbury's nephew, Arthur Balfour, who was resolute in his determination to enforce the law. He believed that 'twenty years of firm government' were needed, and eventually he did succeed in restoring a fair measure of order. When agrarian disorders arose, his response was unwavering, and a demonstration at Mitchelstown, County Cork, was met by police fire resulting in several deaths. 'Remember Mitchelstown' was the Irish cry, and Balfour gained the nickname, 'Bloody Balfour', as a result of the brutal repression.

The policy was accompanied by one of tactful concession for, although Balfour was determined to maintain the status quo in constitutional terms, he was ready to make concessions in an attempt 'to kill Home Rule by kindness'. In the short ministry of 1885, the Conservatives had passed the Ashbourne Act to make loans available for land purchase, and this was extended by Balfour. His 1891 Land Act established a Board to make funds available to those peasants who owned farms which were too small to be farmed economically. The measure was meant to encourage them to increase the size of their holdings, and it also made cheap seed and advice easily available to them.

As far as it went, it was a useful policy offering solid economic advantages, but the long history of neglect and hatred which soured relations between Britain and Ireland could not be overcome by such concessions, however well meant they were. The Catholics of Ireland regarded themselves as a nation who could govern themselves better than the British could. They were looking for the chance to do so and Home Rule was the only concession in which they were really interested.

Chamberlain had left the Liberal government to lead the opposition to the Home Rule Bill. In 1893 he was again the foremost opponent when Gladstone made a second attempt to introduce Home Rule. In the House of Lords, Hartington proposed its rejection and Salisbury spoke up for the Union of Britain and Ireland. The Bill was defeated.

j) Salisbury and Overseas Policy

In the late nineteenth century there were limits beyond which Lord Salisbury's governments would not go in pandering to the desires of the expanded electorate. But if it did not offer jam in the form of social legislation, at least it offered treacle in the form of a sentimental emotional approach to Empire. It was not so much a policy as a way of looking at the world. It emphasised the unrivalled prestige and might of the British Empire, and the force for good that Britain was in the world. It reflected a popular emotion, which made many people feel pride in the fact that God had accorded the British people the privilege of presiding over a quarter of the world, and assuming what the writer Kipling saw as the 'white man's burden'.

The Empire had been one of Disraeli's preoccupations in his Crystal Palace speech, and in the last decades of the century its greatest political exponent was Joseph Chamberlain, the Colonial Secretary after 1895. When he went over to the Conservative side he was able to offer the party the chance to share in his dream, 'To organise an Empire - one may almost say to create an Empire - greater and more potent for peace than any that history has yet known; that is a dream if you like, but a dream of which no man need be ashamed'.

Lord Salisbury was a more cautious imperialist, and was less romantic in his notions. He developed a mastery of the problems involved in the largely peaceful opening up of Africa, and his proven method of firm and patient negotiation suited the situation. He favoured a policy of colonial expansion and believed that it brought benefits both to Britain and to the territories that were added to the Empire. But he preferred commercial penetration to the military conquests of other nations, such as the French. He saw British influence as a 'great civilising Christianising force', with Britain being the territorial guardian under whom native peoples could develop in their own ways. Chamberlain felt similarly, although his speeches placed more emphasis upon the economic benefits of Empire. He was a colonial reformer and also favoured schemes of imperial federation, especially for defence purposes. However, little was achieved in either of these directions, mainly because the policies were inhibited by a lack of Treasury funds, and the Empire developed as a partnership without formal ties.

Imperialism suffered a major setback in the Boer War (1899-1902), which was the culmination of prolonged friction between the British and the Boers in southern Africa. The Boer farmers in the independent republics of the Transvaal and the Orange Free State felt threatened by the British immigrants, whom they called 'Uitlanders', who were flooding into their countries in search of gold and diamonds, and who threatened to outnumber them in the foreseeable future, whilst the settlers felt that their basic rights were being denied. Joseph Chamberlain was widely seen by his critics as a 'warmonger' whose speeches and actions had been provocatively anti-Boer. On neither side was there a spirit of compromise, and war followed.

The Boers gained several initial successes, for they had the advantage of knowing their country well. It required heavy reinforcements in 1900 to turn the tide, and though the British emerged victorious, it was only after the Boers had staged a two year display of effective guerilla warfare. Moreover, in order to win the war, it was seen as necessary to confine the Boer population in special reserves, the first 'concentration camps', and the barbaric methods involved in the fighting, as well as the difficulty in overcoming the Boers, did much to discredit the cause of Imperialism.

Salisbury had had doubts about the conduct of events leading to the war, and disliked its necessity. In overseas matters, his approach was one of peaceful negotiation where possible, and he was noted for his coolness in international disputes - his 'masterly inactivity'. As he put it, 'British policy is to drift lazily down stream, occasionally putting out a boathook to avoid a collision'. He was prepared to 'put out a boathook' if he perceived that, without some initiative, a situation could damage British interests. He was particularly critical of Gladstone's policies between 1880-5 which, he felt, had left the country exposed and alone, and he accused the Liberals of 'uniting the Continent of Europe - against England'. He used the term 'splendid isolation' in discussing his policy, and though he meant it to be a warning about the situation in which Britain might find itself, it has often inaccurately been used to describe his outlook.

In the period up until 1890, he was faced by Bismarck's diplomatic skills. Bismarck was increasing the size of the German army and making a Reinsurance Treaty with Russia in 1887. Salisbury was worried about Russian designs in the Balkans, and a possible threat to the security of the Mediterranean. Therefore, he concluded a series of Mediterranean Agreements with Italy and then Austria, which were vague promises of mutual support, aimed primarily at Russia which, along with France, was seen as a potential enemy. Germany was not viewed as a likely foe at this time, and was keen to conclude an alliance with Britain in 1889, shortly before Bismarck's fall. Salisbury remained wary of formal alliances, of the kind that other Powers were fond of making. He saw them as commitments which could entangle Britain in disputes not of primary concern. However, aware of the growing closeness of the Franco-Russian axis, and of the weakness of British sea-power, his Government passed a Naval Defence Act in 1899 to increase the size and quality of the navy.

The generally peaceful partitioning of the African continent, the skilful resolution of international disputes and the establishment of a strong navy were to his credit, and his period at the helm was one of British strength and power, 'the high tide of British imperialism and power in the world'. The celebration of the Golden and Diamond Jubilees of Queen Victoria in 1887 and 1897 had provided a chance for the nation to bask in national and imperial pride, confident of its place in the world. That confidence was to be dented seriously by the failures of the Boer War. Until then, however, Salisbury's achievements on the global scene were impressive, and as Winston Churchill put it, 'No Foreign Secretary has ever wielded the diplomatic boathook with greater dexterity'.

k) Salisbury's Resignation, and the Premiership of Balfour

At the turn of the century the Conservatives seemed secure. The Khaki Election of 1900 was successfully fought, the Liberals were divided over the war, and there seemed no reason for the long period of Conservative dominance to come to an end. Salisbury stepped down from the premiership in 1902, and the succession was well-timed. He hoped to ease his nephew, Arthur Balfour, into the leadership, and at the time Chamberlain was briefly out of action, having been run over by a passing cab. In any case, although Chamberlain was a more dynamic contender, he was not a true Conservative. He was still a Liberal Unionist, a partner of the official party, but one which retained its separate identity until the reforms of 1911. Many Conservatives would have felt unhappy with an ex-Radical at their head.

Arthur Balfour had many gifts. He possessed a fine intellect and an ability to analyse any problem. He was an amateur philosopher, the author of *A Defence of Philosophical Doubt*, and was according to Lord Birkenhead 'the finest brain that has been applied to politics in our time'. A bachelor of wit, elegance and charm, he was a welcome guest in any English country house where his social gifts went down well. Lloyd George captured something of his rather effeminate style in his dismissive remark that he was 'just like the scent on a pocket handkerchief'. Not for nothing was he known in society as 'Pretty Fanny'!

His wealth and background, his cultural preoccupations, and his languid air made him appealing to those of his own class. He was a 'Conservative's Conservative'. He had much less appeal to the 'man in the street', and showed little awareness of their feelings. As Joseph Chamberlain's eldest son, Austen, observed, 'He has no comprehension of the habits or thoughts of his countrymen, and no idea how things strike them'. He was unusually remote from the problems of everyday life. Neither was he particularly well-suited to the position of party leader. For all of his intellectual excellence and acknowledged ability, he was not to be a success. Within the Cabinet he took open-mindedness too far. It was commendable to see both sides of a question, but unfortunately he seemed unable ever to come down on one side and give a lead. He was open to the charge of indecision, and though he had a certain dexterity in improvisation and surviving scrapes, these were not qualities which inspired the party or the voters. Moreover, he was unsympathetic to the business interest, which was becoming more important in the party.

The 'social question' did not occupy a high place in his thoughts, and unlike Chamberlain he had no great desire to get things done. He could see the problems which demanded attention, but he did not look too hard for solutions to them. He shared his uncle's general distrust of political and economic change. Although he was keen to credit the Conservatives with most of the important reforms of the nineteenth century, he was not the man to embark on many new ones. In tackling any social issue, he stressed the importance of ensuring that individual effort was not discouraged, for he believed that the self-reliance of people who used their talents to the full was the best means of raising the general standard. Neither did he think that one class should benefit from confiscation from another, and he was reluctant to see reform paid for by burdens on his own class. As he later put it, when opposing the Liberal Chancellor of the Exchequer, '... not out of the kind of taxes put on by Lloyd George'.

At the time of his takeover the situation looked promising because he had an overall parliamentary majority and faced a divided and weak opposition. He soon showed unusual tenacity in pushing a controversial Education Bill through the House of Commons. This abolished the School Boards established by the Liberals in 1870 and put elementary education into the hands of elected local councils. It also encouraged Local Education Authorities to 'survey the needs of their area' for secondary education, and enabled them to make technical and even adult provision. The 'Balfour Act' was a landmark in the history of English education, for it not only brought about unified control but for the first time dealt with elementary and higher education together. It was a considerable personal achievement for Morant, the civil servant who largely drafted the Bill, and Balfour, who gave him his whole-hearted backing, and it provided the basic idea for the local administration of education for over 40 years. Yet commendable though the initiative was, Balfour showed insensitivity in his handling of the religious issues which dogged any reform in this area, and antagonised the Nonconformists by offering rate-aid to Church of England schools; in Wales particularly, the Nonconformists kept up strong resistance. They had looked forward to the impending bankruptcy of this sector, and Balfour's measure was to give Church schools new life.

He achieved little else in the social field, other than the Unemployed Workmen Act of 1905, which established Distress Committees in the larger towns to help the unemployed to find work. These Committees were empowered, among other things, to open labour exchanges and to aid emigration, and the ideas the Act represented were in some respects useful. However, they had nothing to offer for many of the unemployed. For many in hardship the last resort remained the hated workhouse system created by the New Poor Law of 1834.

In particular, Balfour was unwilling to address the issues created by a series of legal judgements which cast doubt upon the position in law of the Trade Unions. Disraeli had been happy to restore rights to working men; Balfour offered them little, at a time when workers were anxious about their legal position and right to strike. A decision in the Taff Vale case, upheld by the House of Lords in 1901, had made it clear that a union's funds were liable for civil damages. In other words, unions might have to pay for damages (costs and inconvenience) suffered by an employer because of strike action.

Balfour was similarly insensitive in his reaction to the introduction of Chinese labour into South Africa which was again upsetting to the nonconformist conscience and to British workers on economic and humanitarian grounds. Conditions of work there were an affront to liberal and humane people, whilst trade unionists and others particularly dwelt on the terms of pay and employment; some resented the loss of employment opportunities to British workers.

Balfour was more successful in matters of foreign policy and defence. The Anglo-Japanese Treaty of 1902, the creation of the Committee of Imperial Defence, and the introduction of reforms in the army and navy were useful achievements. Moreover, the Land Purchase Act introduced by George Wyndham in 1903 was a beneficial continuation of the Conservative policy of 'killing Home Rule by kindness', and did much finally to resolve the land question in Ireland by enabling many tenants to become peasant proprietors as a result of long-term loans at low rates of interest. However, the issue which dominated his administration and seriously split the Conservative Party was that of tariff reform.

l) The Tariff Reform Controversy

Joseph Chamberlain, still at the Colonial Office, had a vision of imperial strength based on some kind of a federal structure, underpinned by military unity and a customs union. Over the former he was thwarted by other statesmen at the Colonial Conference of 1902 which he chaired. But in 1903 he put forward a bold scheme for tariff reform which in reality meant a return to protectionism. Disraeli, the earlier Tory advocate of protection, had been converted to free trade and this policy had been the accepted orthodoxy in both parties ever since. Now Chamberlain was talking of retaliatory tariffs against those countries which applied duties against British goods, and of imperial preference, a policy by which Britain and the dominions gave each other preferential rates of duties so that Commonwealth trade was promoted at the expense of trade with other countries.

In so doing, Chamberlain took up an issue which was not to be resolved within the party for another three decades. It was an issue which never provided the Conservatives with any electoral advantage, and on occasion did them much harm. The immediate impact of his move was to rally the disunited Liberals and open a serious breach in the Conservative Party. Some government supporters, such as the old Whig, Lord Hartington, now the Duke of Devonshire, were in favour of free trade. More, perhaps one third of the parliamentary party, were in agreement with Chamberlain, and many more were in the middle, like Balfour himself. He inclined to Chamberlain's view, but felt that the issue was better taken up after an election, for it was bound to damage party unity.

Balfour tried to hold the ring and keep his Cabinet and party together but Chamberlain was not to be silenced. The result was that in September 1903 several ministers, including Chamberlain and Hartington, left the government. Chamberlain sought to rally the country in support of his new cause. He knew that he needed working-class support, but workers were suspicious of the benefits which he claimed for tariff reform. He argued that opening up colonial trade would provide greater employment opportunities in the Empire. He also said that if British firms were less exposed to competition, then home industry would flourish. From the prosperity so generated, the government would finance social reform. Workers had no reason to believe that a Unionist government under Balfour would offer much in the way of social reform, and there was no guarantee that the prospects of greater employment would come about. On the other hand, more expensive food would be a reality. Tariffs on imported corn would mean dearer bread, as Liberals reminded the electorate in posters depicting the large loaf they could have with Free Trade, and the smaller one under Chamberlain's scheme.

HISTORY REVERSES ITSELF;
OR, PAPA JOSEPH TAKING MASTER ARTHUR A PROTECTION WALK.

Papa Joseph. "COME ALONG, MASTER ARTHUR. *DO* STEP OUT!"
Master Arthur. "THAT'S ALL VERY WELL, BUT YOU KNOW I CANNOT GO AS FAST AS YOU DO."

History Reverses itself, Punch *cartoon, 1903*

Balfour was in a difficult position. The Conservative cause was bitterly divided, and his attempt to placate all elements and keep the party together was understandable. But he was left looking indecisive. A contemporary ditty outlined his position,

> I'm not for Free Trade, and I'm not for Protection
> I approve of them both, and to both have objection.

m) The 1906 Election

In December 1905, well before it was necessary, Balfour had had enough and resigned. The in-coming Liberal administration quickly called an election for January. This was to be disastrous for the Conservatives, yielding their lowest total of MPs for many years. The Liberals had an overwhelming majority over all parties, and they were likely to gain Irish and Labour support. To Balfour perhaps the most ominous portent in the election was the arrival of 53 Labour/Lib-Lab MPs - 'the cork bobbing on the socialist tide'.

Why were the Unionists so savaged at the polls?

Balfour's government had started with some advantages, but it also had what Winston Churchill described as 'an exhausted inheritance'. The Party had been long in office, and the 'time for a change' argument was a strong one. Moreover, the Liberals, united by various Unionist actions, now looked in better shape. The Education and Chinese Slavery issues had rallied the nonconformists to their side.

Party organisation had been allowed to run down (see page 143), and the creaking machine made it more difficult for them to maximise their vote in several parts of the country. Neither did the staggering of elections over three weeks help, for the early results in free-trade Lancashire registered a strong swing to the Liberals which voters elsewhere were aware of when they made their choice.

Two issues stand out. The dissension in the party over tariff reform created a seriously damaging image, and, in any case, the policy lacked public appeal. Yet perhaps more important was Tory neglect of the social question, for this election was the first since the last extension of the vote in which there was no distracting issue like Home Rule or the Boer War. Working people had 'come of age', and were looking for improvements in their living and working conditions. Whereas the Liberals made some vague promises of social improvement, the Conservatives offered little and the failure to reverse the Taff Vale Judgement cost them dear.

Chamberlain is often blamed for the Unionist defeat, and there is no doubt that his insistence on taking up the tariff question was electorally harmful. He must share some collective blame for the failure to reverse the Taff Vale decision, for his reforming vision did not embrace the rights of trade unions. However, he had warned Balfour about the dangers the Education Act would cause, and, by then out of office, had opposed Chinese Slavery. He had also urged that the election be called earlier, and certainly the longer it was delayed the more damaging was the internal feuding.

Chamberlain had the satisfaction of seeing a majority of his supporters returned in the election, for it was established that there were 109 Chamberlainites, and only 16 'Free Fooders'. His own and other seats in Birmingham were held against the tide, as was his son's, in Worcester. The Chamberlains were keen party organisers, and never allowed their local machinery to atrophy as happened in other parts of the country. Even more satisfying, whilst he was handsomely re-elected, Balfour and some other Cabinet Ministers were defeated, and for a few weeks he led the party in opposition. If he had wanted to he could probably have seized the leadership, but by 1906 he was too fatigued and had lost the appetite for battle. Soon afterwards, he had left the political scene after suffering a stroke.

n) The Tories in Opposition, 1905-14

The Liberals were in command of the House of Commons, but were in a serious minority in the House of Lords. Very soon, they ran into difficulty with their programme of legislation, and the key to their problem lay in a little-noticed speech of Balfour early in 1906. In it he made his intentions clear; 'The great Unionist Party should still control, whether in power or whether in opposition, the destinies of this great Empire'. He later told Landsdowne, the party leader in the Lords, that 'The two Houses shall not work as separate armies, but shall co-operate in a common plan of campaign'.

The Conservatives regarded themselves as the natural rulers of the nation, and seemed intent on governing whether they were in or out of office. The party was in a negative frame of mind, and this period was one of the least attractive in its history. Racked by continuing dissension over Tariff Reform, the party opposed most of the changes which the Liberals proposed, especially Old Age Pensions and National Insurance against sickness and unemployment - policies which they regarded as confiscation of property rights and a threat to any idea of individual responsibility. Most of the Conservatives in the House of Lords rejected Lloyd George's radical Budget of 1909, which had been skilfully framed so that it would appear that by opposing it, the peers were acting in defence of their own privileges and interests.

The outcome of the Lords' rejection was a Constitutional Crisis, involving two elections in 1910, in which the Conservatives improved their position and the Liberals lost their overall majority. They continued to govern only with Irish and Labour support. The result was that the Liberals produced a Parliament Bill in 1910 which sought to curtail the powers of the Upper House. Balfour accepted that the Budget must pass, and tried to be constructive in discussions with Asquith (the Liberal Prime Minister) over the powers of the House of Lords. Other Unionists were less willing to compromise, and became scornful of his more reasonable approach. They began to mutter 'BMG', Balfour Must Go. The days of the 'Hotel Cecil', as the Balfour-Salisbury family faction was known, were numbered.

o) Events in Ireland

Dependent on Irish support in the House of Commons, the Liberal government came under pressure to revive the issue of self-government for Ireland, the policy of Home Rule which had lain dormant since 1894. Now that the Lords had lost its permanent veto over legislation, the Liberals had no excuse for not making a third bid, and they drew up a Home Rule Bill in 1912. This provoked a second serious constitutional battle, for the Liberal Bill again made no separate provision for the Protestants of Ulster who feared that their interests would be overridden in a predominantly Catholic parliament. As long ago as 1885 Lord Randolph Churchill had warned that 'Ulster will fight, and Ulster will be right'. His words came true for now that there was no barrier to the passage of a Home Rule Bill the fears of Ulstermen increased and they were determined to resist.

Balfour had resigned in November 1911 when it was clear that the whispering campaign against his leadership showed no sign of abating. His successor, Andrew Bonar Law, was a man of very different background and style. He was a shrewd businessman with a good head for statistics. He had developed a mastery of the details of Tariff Reform, of which he was in favour, and of the Ulster issue, on which he held firm, indeed unmovable, beliefs. He was strongly identified with the Ulster cause, at the very time when the situation there was becoming acute. He held his views sincerely, and with deadly earnest; 'These people are prepared to die for their convictions'. He sympathised with those convictions, for he had a Scottish Presbyterian background himself, and therefore shared a similar set of narrow Protestant beliefs.

When the Ulster Volunteers were formed to resist Home Rule, the Unionists gave them their backing. Bonar Law bluntly said that he could not imagine any 'length of resistance to which Ulster can go in which I should not be prepared to support them'. This was perilously close to supporting rebellion, and in so aligning himself with the extremists he was placing the Unionist Party, normally so proud of its reputation as the party of law and order, on the side of those who ignored the rule of law. He was echoing the mood of frustration in a party which had been defeated three times in four years at the polls, and which had ultimately been forced to swallow the Budget and the Parliament Bill. They could not stomach another climbdown. The beginning of the First World War saved the day in this respect at least, for although the Home Rule Bill became law, it was suspended for the duration of international hostilities, and an all-out constitutional crisis thus averted.

p) Women and the Vote

Edwardian politics were turbulent and the threat to parliamentary government was wide-ranging. However, unlike the crises over the Budget and Home Rule, the issue of women's rights was to cut across party lines.

Women were unable to vote in parliamentary elections, although they were allowed to in local government elections. They could serve on school boards after 1870; from 1907 they could sit on county and county borough councils. This degree of local involvement was accepted by many men because they thought that local politics directly affected women's domestic concerns by dealing with such issues as the education of their children. However, no progress had been made on 'votes for women' in parliamentary elections. John Stuart Mill had tried to get the female franchise written into the 1867 Bill but had not succeeded, and in the years afterwards the campaigning of the National Union of Women's Suffrage Association had not brought any reward. In 1903 the Women's Social and Political Union began to attract public attention because of the militancy of its members who resorted to direct action to boost their cause. These Suffragettes, as they were known, expected politicians to declare themselves for or against women's right to vote. The issue provoked major disagreements within each of the parties.

Opinion among rank and file Conservatives was generally hostile to the women's cause and particularly to the methods of the WSPU. The leadership were generally more sympathetic. As long ago as 1848 Disraeli had referred to the 'justice of the women's cause' but in 1867, when piloting his Bill through the House, he offered personal sympathy, but would not commit his party to action. This was typical of subsequent behaviour. The Conservatives gave expressions of support while in opposition, but did nothing when the party was in office.

Lord Salisbury supported women's suffrage, believing that 'by knowledge, by training and by character, women had much to contribute, especially in the fields of morality and religion'. Balfour was more strongly sympathetic, and often spoke in favour in the House of Commons. Yet in the long period of almost uninterrupted Tory rule from 1885 to 1905 both of them were unwilling to press the issue because of backbencher opposition; ultimately, they did not consider it sufficiently important to merit action. Conservative leaders tended to see this as a distracting question, which would arouse much opposition within the party, without bringing tangible gains.

3 Organisational Matters

Lord Randolph Churchill realised the importance of ensuring that the party in London was in touch with the party in the country. He wanted to see Conservatism develop as a popular movement and argued for a bold approach to make it more democratic. It particularly concerned him that the leadership did not reflect the increasingly middle-class composition of many Associations. However, many leading Conservatives were uneasy at this change of character in party membership. They wished to cling to their positions. When Churchill was elected as Chairman of the National Union, and was in a position to challenge party control, he was involved in a behind-the-scenes struggle with the elements who wished to resist change, whom he described as 'the old men crooning over the fire at the Carlton Club'. At one point he resigned and was reinstated with acclaim, a precedent which did not recur when he resigned from the Salisbury government in 1886.

Ultimately he was more interested in policy than organisation, and before the 1885 election he made his peace with Salisbury. He ceased to promote internal party democracy in return for greater recognition of his talents within the leadership. The issue had given him a chance to raise his profile and to gain publicity, and he was content to drop it when it had served its purpose. Perhaps he was aware that if he reached the position of Leader, he might not appreciate any attempt by the mass of the party to be closely involved in policy formulation.

As it was, Salisbury placed reform of the party organisation in the capable hands of Richard Middleton and yielded nothing on the formation of party policy. The central machinery was to operate smoothly over the next seventeen years, and its efficient functioning helped the party to win four of the five elections following Middleton's appointment. On his resignation in 1903, dissension was rife and the lack of harmony between those in charge aggravated Conservative problems in the run-up to the 1906 debacle.

a) The Party in the Country

Salisbury accepted the need for the party to respond to the extensions of the franchise in 1867 and 1884. He approved of the network of Conservative working men's clubs which was being created around the country, and came to see that a mass Conservative movement under the watchful eye of the party elders could prove most beneficial in mobilising support for the party. In particular, he showed interest in another organisation with which Churchill had been involved, the Primrose League. The League was dedicated to upholding the Church, the Constitution and the traditional national virtues, as well as perpetuating the memory of its hero, Disraeli. In its early days it was much influenced by Churchill's personality and outlook, but it gradually developed its own distinctive ethos. It was generally loyal to the leadership and did much to arouse an interest in the party's affairs. It organised many social events, such as concerts and entertainments, and women played a significant role in them. Membership grew rapidly, especially in rural areas, and was fuelled by anti-Home Rule feeling and the new emphasis upon the imperial theme. The League soon developed widespread support around the country, bringing together people from different walks of life in an organisation which encouraged them to work with another for the good of the party.

Another vehicle for the expression of Conservative feeling was the Tariff Reform League through which Chamberlain tried to convert the country to the cause of protectionism and imperial preference. The movement received its initial impetus from the Birmingham Tariff Committee, in which local businessmen were prominent. A national body was rapidly established and soon the London headquarters was co-ordinating branches up and down the country. Mass rallies and smaller meetings were held, and the body exploited the new techniques of popular communication, using songs, records, plays and leaflets to get its message across.

b) The Organisational Reforms of 1911

Defeat is often a spur to organisational improvement, and following the electoral setbacks of 1910 Balfour appointed an enquiry into the whole structure of the Party. The outcome was an amalgamation of the Liberal Unionists and Conservatives, to give the party its modern title, the Conservative and Unionist Party. The relationship of each branch of the machinery to other ones was finally clarified, particularly that between Central Office and the National Union. The new office of Party Chairman was created, and he was to become the head of Central Office, which was given full control over organisation and publicity. The Chief Whip lost any wider organisational duties, and the National Union was to be an influential medium of two-way communication between the country and the leadership, but not a body exercising power.

Making notes on '*Conservatives and Unionists, 1881-1914*'

'A' Level questions relate mainly to the Salisbury and Balfour Governments in this period. Use the following headings to help you recall the information on Salisbury and his work:

Churchill; refer to his Dartford Speech, Tory Democracy, the rift with Salisbury and why he fell;
Salisbury; his attitude to political and social change;

The main measures of his Second and Third Administration, especially the County Councils Act and those on education; Salisbury, Balfour and Ireland; examine the Conservative approach and the main measures; Salisbury and world affairs; his attitude and skill, the 'opening up of Africa', the Boer War and its importance.

On Balfour, write notes on:

His approach to reform; The main measures, such as Education, Defence and Ireland; Problems faced by the Balfour Government, including Taff Vale, Chinese Slavery and particularly Tariff Reform - why it was wanted, its alleged benefits and the divisions it aroused; The 1906 election; the extent of the Conservative defeat. You would do well to make a list of possible contributory factors.

Having now studied the history of the party since Disraeli's death, it is

Summary - Conservatives and Unionists, 1881-1914

worth writing a paragraph or two to summarise the main features of Conservative policy in the period. You might go on to make a list of the features which the Disraelian party and the party post-Disraeli had in common. In so doing, you will be able to come to a judgement as to whether the Disraelian legacy long survived his passing.

***Answering essay questions on** 'Conservatives and Unionists, 1881-1914'*

Despite the length of the period and the prolonged Conservative ascendancy between 1886 and 1905, examiners have tended to neglect this part of the syllabus. Occasionally questions have been set on the career and importance of Lord Randolph Churchill, in which the Fourth Party, the battle between Churchill and the Conservative establishment, their differing conceptions of Conservatism and his fall are all important aspects.

More usually the topic on which questions have been set is Salisbury's record in domestic policy. You may be asked to comment on the view that the second administration was 'solid but unspectacular' - a judgement which it is difficult to dissent from - or that overall the Salisbury years were 'sterile' ones in home affairs. When answering such questions you can enliven your essay by drawing attention to Conservatives such as Churchill, or the Liberal Unionist Chamberlain, who wanted a more enterprising approach than that favoured by Salisbury who preferred a 'quiet life'.

Many examination questions invite you to agree with a quotation such as, in this case, 'solid and spectacular'. Try to be critical in your approach to such judgements. Outright hostility to the observation may be rather risky, unless you are very sure of your ground; it is unlikely that the Chief Examiner has made up or used a remark which is totally without foundation. Simple endorsement of the comment suggests that you lack a mind of your own, and feel unsafe in venturing an opinion. Therefore, the wise stance is to 'broadly agree but ...', or to 'disagree, on balance'. Weigh up the evidence, and then come to your verdict.

Questions are often asked about Balfour, perhaps asking for a discussion of a quotation such as, 'Given the problems which Balfour faced, his administration had some distinguished achievements to its credit between 1902 and 1905'. Here, you would need to discuss the difficulties - the 'exhausted inheritance', Taff Vale, Chinese Slavery and the issue of Tariff Reform - and assess the achievements, such as the Education Act. The voters appear to have been unimpressed with his 'achievements' in 1906; or was he paying the price for a long period of Conservative rule, and the electorate simply felt it was 'time for a change'?

A popular theme among Chief Examiners concerns the causes of the 1906 election defeat, and you could be invited to allocate the blame for the debacle between Balfour and Chamberlain. Why could Chamberlain be held responsible, and on which policies can he be acquitted of guilt? Make a list of those issues on which Chamberlain was, or was not, blameworthy. Try to come to a judgement on which were the overriding reasons for the massive rejection of Unionist policies and personalities. How relevant was the point made above, about the long Conservative ascendancy, or was the electorate, with its large working-class element, now looking for something more from any government than Balfour was willing to give?

Source-based questions on 'Conservatives and Unionists, 1881-1914'

1 Athwart the Course, 1883
Study the cartoon on page 119. Answer the following questions.
a) Who was in charge of the boat marked 'Government' (top left) and who was the leader of the other party's boat? (2 marks)
b) What is the cartoonist implying about the behaviour of Churchill? In what ways was this comment justified? (5 marks)
c) Why did Churchill decide to 'do his own thing' during this period? (3 marks)

2 The Churchill-Salisbury Rift, 1886
Carefully read the three extracts on pages 125-6. Answer the following questions.
a) From the evidence of his letter to Cranborne, why do you think that Salisbury tolerated the presence of Churchill in the government? (3 marks)
b) Using evidence from all of the extracts, suggest why Salisbury found Churchill such a difficult colleague. (4 marks)
c) Based on evidence from their correspondence, what differing expectations did Churchill and Salisbury have of what Conservatism might achieve? (5 marks)
d) How far were the differences between Salisbury and Churchill more ones of style than substance? (8 marks)

3 History Reverses Itself, 1903
Carefully examine the cartoon on page 138 and, if necessay, refer back to chapter 4. Answer the following questions.
a) What two divisive issues were being alluded to in the cartoon? Identify the four characters in the main drawing and inset. (6 marks)
b) Explain the title of the cartoon. (2 marks)
c) What set of proposals was the dominant figure in the foreground keen to see the party take up ? Why did he believe in them? (5 marks)
d) Which of the two issues referred to in the cartoon had the greater effect on the Conservative Party? Explain your answer. (7 marks)

CHAPTER 7

Conclusion

In 1815 the Tories began our period with a prolonged spell in government. In 1914 they were in opposition and had recently suffered three successive election defeats. Yet, despite their ailing fortunes in Edwardian Britain, the Party had generally done well in elections between 1815 and 1914. After a lean generation following the fall of Peel they had come to dominate the last three decades of the century. They had tasted the success of almost 50 years of single-party government and above all had survived into a more democratic age. That, in itself, was a tribute to their power of adaptation, for landed parties of the Right, dedicated to preserving the interests of privilege and property, largely fizzled out in continental Europe. In Britain not only did Conservatism survive, it also flourished. This was in spite of the fact that the vote was extended to working people who formed a majority of the electorate. Their class interests did not at first sight appear to coincide with those of the Conservatives.

1 The Situation in 1914

The Unionist record in opposition after 1906 was not impressive and much energy was dissipated on the disagreements over tariff reform and on internal party manoeuvres. After 1911 the new leadership did spend more time harassing the government and this helped to hold the party together. But it was a unity based on negation, for little thought had gone into formulating a Conservative approach to the great issues of the day, particularly the social one.

Although many Unionists were hopeful of victory in the next election, whenever that might be, after the erosion of Liberal support in 1910 and in subsequent by-elections, they could of course not be certain. In electoral terms they had recovered well, but they would still be dependent on Liberal mistakes and divisions and on the unpopularity of the government over the Ulster question to get them back into power. And the Liberals could not be under-estimated. Despite their problems they were resilient, and there were able men in their ranks whose resourcefulness was not to be doubted.

a) What were the sources of Conservative strength in 1914?

The Party had some things going very much in its favour. Although it was in a minority in the House of Commons, it remained in control of the House of Lords where there was a massive in-built Conservative majority. It is true that the second chamber had lost its permanent veto, but the Conservatives could still use it to delay radical measures of which they strongly disapproved.

In the country Unionist support was strong in certain areas, notably in the cathedral cities, seaside towns and rural areas, and, thanks to the impact of the Chamberlains, in the West Midlands. The Conservatives had become the predominant English party after 1885 and their opponents were increasingly identified with the Celtic fringe. In 1906 this predominance had been shattered, but elections before and after resulted in a Unionist majority among the English constituencies.

English Seats in the House of Commons

	Conservative	Liberal
1885	213	238
1886	322	122
1892	261	190
1895	343	112
1900	332	121
1906	122	306
1910 Jan	233	188
1910 Dec	234	186

In local government the Unionists were well-established. After the creation in 1888 of the new system of elected county councils, political contests gradually crept in. Far from the outcome being beneficial to 'radical spendthrifts', as some Tories had feared, many of those elected were landlords who had previously served their area as magistrates. Counties adjacent to industrial areas returned more businessmen, but they also leaned to the Conservative side.

Unionists were active in other prominent positions in society. They heavily outnumbered the Liberals in the magistracy, to an extent that even some Conservatives found hard to defend. Magistrates were appointed only from men of wealth and substance. Before 1886 such men had been as likely to be Liberals as Conservatives, many of them still finding their loyalties with the forces of change rather than with those of resistance, but the crisis over the future of Ireland in the 1880s was a convenient opportunity for property-owners to switch over on a patriotic issue. Henceforth, the overwhelming weight of property was on the Conservative side.

The same was true in the world of commerce. In the City, the financial centre of London, the Conservatives were favoured by the 'money men' who liked their more cautious approach to public expenditure and their preference for lower taxation of the rich. The press also gave them strong support. The older provincial and pro-Liberal press of the 1850s and 1860s had been losing its popularity, and the new London-based 'nationals' were usually on the Conservative side. Liberal support in the newspaper columns ebbed away significantly after the Home Rule controversy of the 1880s.

In organisational terms the Conservatives were well-equipped and effective. Even if the machinery had been allowed to run-down in 1906, after years in which success had perhaps come too easily, by 1914 it was in better shape. The internal reforms shortly before the First World War had greatly improved efficiency. There was a network of Conservative Clubs and Associations, and the Primrose League had a mass membership of 800,000, including many women, even if it was by then more of a congenial political and social gathering than a serious political force. These were all signs of solid Conservative strength and, although the leadership of Andrew Bonar Law was unimpressive, the party did not lack effective spokesmen in the House of Commons.

b) The Composition of Conservatism

In the nineteenth century Conservatism had undergone a number of changes as it sought to adapt to alterations in electoral conditions. What sort of people were to be found within the Conservative Party in parliament and the country, and whose interests did they represent?

At the beginning of our period, the Party was overtly one of landed property. Within parliament the typical Tory MP was a member of the country gentry. By 1914 this was not so. From the time of Gladstone's leadership of the Liberal Party, but especially after 1885, many members of the middle classes went over to the Conservative side. In the 1885 election for the first time there were more MPs returned representative of industrial and commercial property than of landed property, and it was to be within the Conservative Party that the rise in numbers was most evident.

Occupations of Conservative (and in 1900 Liberal Unionist) MPs

	landed %	industrial/commercial %	professional %
1868	46	31	9
1885	23	50	16
1900	20	52	18

The majority of middle-class MPs were still Liberals and the 1906 House of Commons which they so dominated has been called 'the first middle-class parliament'. But there is no doubt that by the late-Victorian and Edwardian periods the composition of the Conservative Party had significantly altered. The backgrounds of the Unionist members elected in the second election of 1910, when both parties gained broadly equal representation, illustrated the nature of the change. The new parliament was solidly upper and middle class in origin, with business interests having become even more important. One hundred and ninety-six Unionists had been to public schools (90 to Eton), whilst only 23 had a purely secondary education. By occupation, the Unionists comprised:

Financial	124
Landowners	123
Barristers/solicitors	66
Transport Industries	48
Heavy Industries	43
Merchants	20
Coalowners	10
Textiles	5

(Some MPs are counted twice, where they had overlapping interests.)

This change in the type of representation was not confined to the House of Commons. Of the peerages created between 1886 and 1914, more were awarded to business than to landed Conservatives. As the longest-serving Conservative Prime Minister in that period, it was the Marquess of Salisbury, himself the supreme example of the traditional governing classes, who nominated many of the new creations to the Upper House. It would, of course, be wrong to draw too sharp a distinction between the Conservatives of landed backgrounds and those with a middle-class one, for many of the landowners in both Houses were owners of industrial concerns or had substantial share-holdings in them.

Nonetheless, the Unionist Party at Westminster, with its strong industrial and business element, was a very different body from the old Tory party of Lord Liverpool, and the change in composition was not without its tensions. Whereas in the 1840s the conflict between old Toryism and new Conservatism had been difficult to reconcile within the same party, the party before 1914 represented a broad spread of landed and other property. Yet there was still some ill-feeling, for members of the old ruling class felt that their traditional values and approach were under challenge. Lord Hugh Cecil, the son of Lord Salisbury, particularly despised Joseph Chamberlain as a man who had made his fortune in industry, and disapproved of much that he represented. The Cecil family disliked his whole approach to politics, and he remarked that, 'It appears to be utterly sordid and materialistic, not yet corrupt but on the high road to corruption'.

This change in composition to embrace the industrialist class was reflected in the Cabinet. In the nineteenth century Cabinets were well-stocked with country gentlemen, members of the landlord class. Some may have sprung from a commercial background but by the time they entered government they had bought themselves a seat in the country and had left their origins behind. Even the Disraeli Cabinet of 1874 had contained 10 aristocrats out of 17 members - and the rest were upper middle class. After this, Conservative Cabinets included more middle-class representation, albeit rather upper middle class. The Salisbury and Balfour Cabinets comprised a mixture of traditional aristocrats and lawyers and businessmen. They were a little less patrician, although the vast majority had been to public school and Oxbridge and were sufficiently wealthy that they did not need to work in paid employment. In the Balfour cabinet, in 1902, nine members were aristocrats, ten came from the upper middle classes, 16 had been to a public school, (9 to Eton), 14 had been to a university, (13 to Oxbridge).

At the very top, leaders such as Salisbury and Balfour came from traditional ruling families. Both were men of high social standing and wealth who had long been involved in public life. However, the choice of Bonar Law in 1911 seemed to acknowledge the position of 'new wealth' within Conservatism. As an iron merchant, he symbolised the forces of business, and his type of background was to become more common over the next generation, with twentieth-century leaders such as Baldwin and Neville Chamberlain having a similar background.

At all levels in the party, from those near the leadership to those who held key positions in the party machine at Westminster and in the country, the old style of Conservative was still well-represented. But these men were supplemented by new men whose approach was different. They were a useful addition in that they provided the party with new funds.

The changing composition was not surprising, for at the end of the century the economic situation of the country was undergoing change. The landlord class had been seriously hit by the 'Great Depression' of the late-nineteenth century, for they had suffered acutely from the easy availability of cheap imported food from overseas. Prices of wheat and meat had dropped, and the amount of land given over to arable and dairy farming had declined. Many of the country gentry had seen their wealth reduced, and their significance in the national economy gradually declined. Britain had rapidly industrialised, and it was now industry and trade which were the most important forms of capital.

What had happened by the end of our period was that the forces of property of whatever type had gone over to the Conservative side. On the one hand, the Conservatives had gained the business element which had previously felt better-represented by the Liberals. Also, much of the landed element within the Liberal Party, mainly Whigs, had deserted and gone over to their rivals; Lord Hartington (the Duke of Devonshire) was one such example. Conservatism in 1914, therefore, included old and new wealth, and in its membership had become the party for many men of title and affluence.

c) A Party for the Working Classes?

Conservatism in the nineteenth century was never restricted to the wealthy. Especially after 1867 this vote was too narrow to provide victory on its own, and needed reinforcement. It was important for the Conservatives to be successful in gaining some support from members of the lower-middle and working classes. In the redistribution of seats made for the 1885 election several new constituencies had been created in large towns and cities. Previously Conservative voters had been heavily outnumbered in those areas, for they were dominated by workers in the poorer central parts, but now they were able to gain representation. Lord Salisbury had noted that there was 'a great deal of villa Toryism which requires organisation', and certainly the Conservatives began to gain much support in the better-off suburbs. Their efficient electoral machine enabled them to organise campaigns carefully, and particularly in London their 30 full-time party agents (as against the Liberals' three) were effective in winning support among the labouring classes.

The Conservatives regularly obtained one third or more of working-class votes. By 1914 they received considerable support from those who were swayed by deference, who felt that the Conservatives were the natural party of government and had the leaders 'born to rule'. For instance, they performed impressively in rural areas where there was solid Conservative leadership in the community from the country gentry, on the Bench and in local government. They also did better where class solidarity was less apparent. Where there was no strong middle-class presence - Scotland, Wales and the north of England - they were less successful, for these were predominantly areas where class antagonism could be significant. Where there was a solid middle-class interest some workers were keen to identify with it, perhaps wishing to upgrade themselves socially. Voting Conservative was a way of keeping up with the Joneses.

Lancashire was one working-class area where there was strong Conservative support. Hostility to the Irish immigrants in the large cities there was a factor, and the Liberals suffered from their identification with this group. The Conservatives made a conscious and untypical attempt to organise the industrial labourers of the North-west, for the party leaders encouraged the formation of Conservative Workingmen's Clubs alongside the more exclusively middle-class Constitutionalist Associations. Disraeli had been wary of allowing separate organisations for working men.

In London the Conservatives similarly benefited from fears aroused by immigration, in this case of the large number of Jews who came to England in the late-nineteenth and early-twentieth century. Party propaganda was effective in painting a picture of the Conservatives as the party of English nationalism, of Monarchy, of Empire and of

Protestantism. It combined these elements together to create an image of patriotism, and in the Boer War had the ideal opportunity to appeal for re-election, 'not as Conservatives, not as politicians, but as Englishmen'.

The Conservative working-class vote was, then, often deferential and/or patriotic. It was also based on economic self-interest, for some artisans considered that the party had a better understanding of their needs. Skilled working men, who had been employed for the same company for many years, might be promoted to foremen, and were pleased to think of themselves as having middle-class status and saw voting Conservative as an indication of social respectability. Apart from foremen and other overseers of those who actually did the manual work, there was a growing number of office workers, especially in London, who thought of themselves as being lower middle class rather then workers. Such people, often separated into superior neighbourhoods of the large cities, wanted to keep the benefits they possessed, and tended to associate the Conservatives with a good standard of living and plenty of employment. They were also aware of the tradition of paternalistic Conservative social measures, such as slum clearance, worker's accident compensation and other factory protection.

The combination of middle, lower-middle and working-class support provided the Conservatives with a firm electoral base. It was because they gained support from all sections of the community that they could claim that as a party they transcended class divisions. They were truly a 'national' party, whereas the Liberals depended more on the votes of the masses in the towns and cities. Conservatives could claim to speak and act for the nation, and were able to portray themselves as the patriotic party which stood for the interests of the whole community.

d) Attitudes to the Role of the State

There had always been an element of paternalism in Conservative thought. Throughout the nineteenth century, there were Tory thinkers, writers and politicians who accepted the need for state activity. In particular, Lord Shaftesbury, the philanthropist, who as Lord Ashley had been a committed social reformer in the House of Commons between 1822 and 1851, felt a deep sense of moral obligation to those less fortunate than himself. Disraeli and the Young England group wanted to see the palace made safe by keeping the cottage content. Such Tories accepted the inequality which existed in a hierarchical society, but they wished to temper its excesses by tackling the worst abuses.

Since Disraeli there has always been a strain in Conservative thinking which has felt a sense of social obligation for the least privileged. Usually its exponents have sought to combine traditional defence of established institutions with a popular programme of reform. By the late-nineteenth century the question of state intervention was becoming more important because within the Liberal Party people were beginning to wonder whether government should assume a larger role. In 1906 Liberals were still not committed to extensive social reform, but as Lloyd George and Winston Churchill became more influential the party began to promote measures which pioneered the welfare state. How should the Conservatives now feel about such reform? Could they accept the social challenge of these 'New Liberals' and show that they also favoured state action, or should it be opposed?

Whereas Liberals worried about the social question primarily for reasons of conscience, some Conservatives were anxious for a different reason. Various surveys had pointed to the unfitness of the nation, particularly of its working population. This had implications for national defence, and some members of the party saw the need for an improvement in the people's health. They urged Balfour to make local authorities feed necessitous schoolchildren, institute medical tests, and offer some relief to the temporarily unemployed, which he did in 1905. On school meals and tests, he felt that he could be 'as sympathetic as he liked, but there would be no increase in rates'.

Salisbury and Balfour were not in favour of any policy of significant social improvement. Though moderately paternalistic, they nonetheless upheld the rights of property. They accepted a society in which people were unequal as entirely natural. Furthermore, they feared that social reform would threaten the liberty of the individual. Bonar Law showed no greater enthusiasm, believing that people who wanted social reform would not vote Conservative anyway.

Lord Hugh Cecil, himself an MP, explained the thinking of the Conservative establishment in his book *Conservatism*. He related the current situation to the writings of Burke, and warned against any policy which smacked of Jacobinism, and 'the levelling principles of the French Revolution'. He felt that it was 'plain that to take what one man has and to give it to another is unjust, even though the first man be rich and the second man poor'. But could Conservatives support measures designed to help disadvantaged sections of the community, such as the poor, without this infringing on the rights of the rich? He recognised no entitlement on the part of the least well off to receive any help, but accepted that there could well be reasons for the state helping them. Charity, gratitude for services rendered and expediency might be such motives, and Conservatism could encompass all three of them. Cecil was willing to justify state help, but had no wish to see it develop along socialist lines for socialism involved 'the end of private property, the fall of traditional institutions, the collapse of Christianity, and the disruption of morality and family life'.

Reform which did not threaten established institutions and rights of property, and was relatively cheap, could have a place in Conservative thinking. Indeed, it might be right and prudent to go along with it. However, the scope of such change was likely to be rather limited. When it came to responding to specific measures, Lord Hugh Cecil and his Conservative colleagues in the House could agree that the proposals should be viewed on their individual merits.

Joseph Chamberlain had met with little Conservative support when he put forward a scheme for old age pensions at the end of the nineteenth century, but he never gave up the idea. However, his increasing preoccupation with South African questions meant that the issue was no longer high on his list of priorities. In any case, the cost of the Boer War made any action very unlikely. Balfour felt able to say that 'Joe's war had stopped Joe's pensions'. Although the party leadership acted tactically and tried to make the Liberal attempt of 1908 to introduce old age pensions unworkable by widening its costs, for thinkers such as Cecil the issue was the more traditional one. Pensions might 'weaken the fibre of the people', and therefore might seriously undermine the capacity to resist aggression in any future war.

e) The Conservative Approach

When reviewing their history Conservatives like to see themselves as a party committed to peaceful change. They pride themselves on their patriotism and support for great institutions, and they like to point to the tradition of Tory Democracy, that legacy of Disraeli which still inspires many Conservatives today. These have been continuous themes in Conservative literature.

For a Conservative reviewing the situation in 1900, it was a matter of pride that the constitution had been preserved. The House of Lords still retained significant powers and had the ability to block measures which were considered too dangerous or too radical. The Church of England was still the established church in England, Scotland and Wales, the Union with Ireland was still in place, and the monarchy was secure. Of course, there had been necessary adaptations, of which Conservatives had sometimes been the instigators, as in 1867 over parliamentary reform, but there had been no revolutionary change.

In 1914 the situation looked less certain. The House of Lords had lost its permanent veto over legislation, the Welsh Church had been disestablished and Home Rule for Ireland was on the statute book, even if it was suspended for the duration of the war. Moreover, in the process, the country had undergone a constitutional crisis over the rights of the Second Chamber and Ireland had been taken to the brink of civil war over Home Rule. On both these issues, the Conservatives had acted in a way which jeopardised their claim to be the party of law and order.

In defending the constitution, Conservatives have wished to look after the interests of those who are protected by it. This involves many of the forces of rank and property who looked to Conservatism as a guarantor of their position. Yet if resistance to change and defence of self-interest have been an element in the party's history, it has always shown some shrewdness in knowing when to give way. The traditional element within Conservatism sometimes found it difficult to compromise, but usually some of its more far-sighted leaders have recognised the importance of broadening the electoral appeal and social base of the cause they represent.

Writers such as Coleman have stressed the conservatism of Conservatism, seeing it more as reaction tempered by an instinct for self-preservation. Speaking of the party in 1900, he depicted it as 'still a party of resistance and survival, of obstruction and delay and, when necessary, of compromise in order to avoid worse'. More obviously sympathetic writers such as Lord Hugh Cecil, have also felt that change has too often come at the last moment. In *Conservatism*, he reviewed four great events of the nineteenth century which in his view were disastrous for the party. On the first three, Roman Catholic emancipation, the Reform Bill of 1832 and the repeal of the Corn Laws, he found his predecessors guilty of failing to promote gradual change when it was still possible. The timing of change was all-important, and for him on these occasions action was taken too late; on the fourth issue, the 1867 Reform Act, he felt that the measure was passed with too much haste!

There were times when the mood of MPs was to resist the tide of political and social progress, times when self-interest was placed before the interests of the whole community. Fortunately for the party, on both occasions a Peel or a Disraeli was on hand to reorganise the party, refashion its image and provide it with a broader appeal. Their characters and styles were very different, but each was seeking to help the party to adjust to changing conditions, and to commit it to a course of moderate reform. More sophisticated Tories could see the need to recognise the rights of Catholics in 1829, to accept the Reform Bill as 'a final and irrevocable settlement' in 1832, or to abandon agricultural protection in the early 1850s. Sometimes, realism came at the eleventh hour, but nonetheless it came. Adaptation was and has remained a part of Conservative history.

f) Old Toryism and Modern Conservatism

The party is a coalition which does not represent a single class nor a single, galvanising political idea. There was a time when it was to a large extent the political expression of the landed interest, but that was the exception to the rule. The party of Lord Liverpool does not bear a clear resemblance to the one today, for he was the product of an essentially pre-industrial rural society. However, the party of Peel does, for he seemed to represent the new industrial society.

Peel was the first recognisably modern leader, the one who converted Toryism to a policy of moderate, cautious reform. The landed interest was preoccupied with the Church, the position of the monarchy, and the protection of private property. They knew little and cared less about industry. Peel's ministry was concerned with the problems of the Industrial Revolution, and the movement to free trade. Old Toryism was rooted in the feudal tradition, hierarchical, authoritarian and paternalistic. Conservatism was to take that aristocratic and Anglican tradition from the past, and to graft on to it the aspirations of the middle classes. The Conservatives were to become, from Peel's day onwards, the party representing an alliance of the different forms of property - landed, industrial and commercial. By 1914, they were the safe haven for owners of all types of capital, what one writer has called 'a party of property and patriotism'.

Peel's contribution to the development of Conservatism in the nineteenth century was to refashion the party in such a way as to bring its thinking up to date, and to provide a model of constructive opposition and sound, competent administration. He ensured that the party was national in its appeal, and not the preserve of only the landed interest. Disraeli also strongly believed in the need for the United Kingdom to be one nation, and the Tory Party to be national in its embrace. He did something else. As Ian Gilmour, a modern 'wet' Conservative, has discerned, he was 'able to bring warmth to Conservatism, and to add to its basic common sense a degree of romance, generosity and excitement, which ... many Conservatives ... are usually unable to express'. Of the 'basic common sense', there is room for debate. But of all Conservative leaders from the early-nineteenth century up to the outbreak of war in 1914, it was Disraeli who has been the greatest inspiration of the modern party.

Chronological Table

Dates	Leader	Main issues/elections

In Office

1815-27	Liverpool	Post-war 'repression'
		'Liberal phase' in 1820s
1827	Canning	'Liberal' ministry
1827-8	Goderich	Short-lived ministry
1828-30	Wellington	'Iron Duke'
		Catholic Emancipation 1829
		Metropolitan Police 1829

In Opposition

1830-4	Wellington	Opposition to parliamentary reform
		1832 massive election defeat

In Office

1834-5	Peel	Tamworth Manifesto 1835

In Opposition

1835-41	Peel	Electoral recovery 1835 and 1837

In Office

1841-6	Peel	1841 Election victory
		Financial reform, Maynooth,
		Corn Law split

In Opposition

1846-66	Bentinck/Derby	Two brief Derby governments,
	Derby/Disraeli	1852 and 1858-9

In Office

1866-8	Derby/Disraeli	1867 Reform Act
		1868 election defeat

In Opposition

1868-74	Disraeli	1872 Crystal Palace speech;
		restatement of party policy and
		overhaul of organisation
		1874 election victory

In Office

1874-80	Disraeli	Social reforms Assertive overseas policy 1880 election defeat

In Opposition

1880-5	Northcote	Fourth Party

In Office

1885	Salisbury	Minority ministry

In Opposition

1886	Salisbury	first Home Rule Bill

In Office

1886-92	Salisbury	1886 Churchill's resignation Limited reforms

In Opposition

1892-5	Salisbury	second Home Rule Bill

In Office

1895-1902	Salisbury	Boer War (1899-1902) Khaki election of 1900
1902-5	Balfour	1902 Education Act Tariff Reform controversy

In Opposition

1905-11	Balfour	1906 election defeat Tory opposition over 1909 Budget
1911-14	Bonar Law	Ulster opposition to Home Rule

Further Reading

Historians and the Conservative Party

Vast amounts of literature have been written about the political life of the nineteenth century, but the development of political parties throughout the period has been less fully covered. Aspects of Conservatism have been referred to in many books, but no continuous study of the character, personalities, policies and organisation of the party has been attempted - or at least, not at a level which is meaningful to the student at 'A' Level or in the first year in Higher Education.

There are valuable and generally reliable histories of political parties, notably *The Growth of the Party System* by Ivor Bulmer-Thomas, and *British Political Parties* by Robert McKenzie, which are useful for some aspects of the subject. The nearest to a continuous history is Robert Blake's *The Conservative Party from Peel to Churchill,* which does not purport to be a comprehensive analysis of the party's history, but nonetheless is a fascinating book to read, not least because of the parallels it draws with more recent political circumstances. Two other short, but stimulating, works are Frank O'Gorman's *The Emergence of the British Two-party System, 1760-1832* and Eric Evans' *Political Parties in Britain, 1783-1867,* which differ on their view of the extent of party activity in the early period.

The general works on the nineteenth century, such as E.T. Woodward's *The Age of Reform* and R.C.K. Ensor's *England 1870-1914,* are useful volumes for reference, as are the books of Asa Briggs and Donald Read in the eleven-volume *A History of England* series produced by Longman. However, for more detailed scholarship, it is the biographies and specialised works which are invaluable. In particular, Gash on Peel, Blake on Disraeli and Robert Rhodes James on Lord Randolph Churchill, throw an illuminating light not only on the persons of whom they write, but on the attitudes and policies of other personalities of the day. H.J. Hanham's study of *Elections and Party Management,* and the works of Paul Smith and E.J. Feuchtwanger on Disraelian Conservatism offer interesting and penetrating analyses of their chosen areas.

Much of the material on Conservatism in the nineteenth century has been written by people who greatly admired their subjects, the obvious example being the massive study of Disraeli by W.F. Monypenny and G. Buckle, once described as 'a quarry and a classic'. It was a sympathetic study, as many older biographies tend to be. It is therefore stimulating to read the work of Bruce Coleman on *Conservatism and the Conservative Party in the Nineteenth Century,* for his judgement is not clouded by any bonds of sentiment towards the party, and he writes as one who sees its raison d'etre as being primarily to defend the self-interest of its members and to hold back social progress and change.

Index